Ways We Worship

William N. McElrath

BARRON'S

All inquiries should be addressed to:
Barron's Educational Series, Inc.
250 Wireless Boulevard
Hauppauge, New York 11788

Library of Congress Catalog Card No. 96-39694

International Standard Book No. 0-8120-6625-1

Library of Congress Cataloging-in-Publication Data

McElrath, William N.
    Ways we worship / by William N. McElrath.
        p.   cm.
    Includes bibliographical references.
    Summary: Describes the basic principles and practices of various
religions throughout the world, including Judaism, Christianity, Islam,
Hinduism, Buddhism, Shintoism, and others.
    ISBN 0-8120-6625-1
    1. Worship—Juvenile literature. 2. Religions—Juvenile literature.
[1. Religions.] I. Title.
BL550.M37   1997
291.3—dc21   96-39694
                                                     CIP
                                                      AC

PRINTED IN THE UNITED STATES OF AMERICA

10 9 8 7 6 5 4 3 2 1

KENNEDY

Table of Contents

🌐 1 Many Ways

Tara strolled toward the activity bus, balancing her schoolbooks on her arm.

"Come on, Tara!" Rebekah called back over her shoulder.

"Cool it, Bekah! What's your hurry?"

"I need to get home before dark," Rebekah urged. "And that's hard to do in winter, with band practice coming after school on Fridays."

Tara frowned. "Surely your mom doesn't worry that much!"

Rebekah shook her head. "It's not that. You see, our day of worship starts at sundown on Friday."

"I thought Jews worshiped on Saturdays," said Tara as she bounced up the high steps onto the bus.

"That's right, we do," Rebekah agreed as she plopped down beside Tara. "But it so happens that we count our days starting with evenings instead of mornings."

Tara turned to look out the dirt-streaked window of the bus. "I'm glad I don't have to go to church till Sunday morning."

"Lucky you!" Kevin put in as he walked up the aisle of the bus. "We're Christians, too, but we go to church on Saturdays." He squeezed in beside Jabar and Nikhil on the seat behind the two girls.

"Well, just to make things more interesting . . .," Jabar chimed in, "our day of worship is on Friday."

"But you have to go to school on Fridays," said Kevin.

Jabar nodded. "On Fridays it's mostly men who go to our place of worship, anyway—not many women, and not many kids like us."

Nikhil shook his head. "I don't see why you have to have a special time or place for worship, anyway. We can worship any time, anywhere!"

Have you ever heard a conversation similar to this one?

Have you ever noticed your neighbors worshiping in ways different from the ways you and your family worship?

Do any of your friends at school wear special clothes or wear their hair in special ways because of their religious beliefs?

Do some of them refuse to eat certain foods because of religious rules?

Do some of them ask to be excused from taking part in certain activities?

"Wait a minute," you may feel like saying. Maybe you've never paid much attention to religion. Maybe you don't think of yourself as being a religious person at all. Maybe you and your family don't follow any of the usual ways of worshiping.

Just the same, you may find this book interesting. Whether we realize it or not, the ways we worship can play a big part in making all of us who we are. Many different religions—in many different countries, at many different times in history—have helped to shape the world as we know it today.

In the twenty-first century, the ways we worship will go right on being one of the most important things that divides all the different people of the world into warring camps . . . or brings them together into peaceful neighborhoods.

WHAT IS WORSHIP?

Why is this book called *Ways We **Worship***? Worshiping isn't the only thing we do when we follow a certain religion. Yet worshiping is an important part of any religion.

Worship takes many forms. If you could see some people worshiping, you might not even recognize that that's what they're doing.

The word *worship* itself comes from an old English word: *worth-ship*. You already know other words like *friendship* and *fellowship*, so you can probably figure out for yourself what *worth-ship* means: having worth or value. Because of that meaning, the word *worship* has come to have this definition:

WORSHIP: How we give honor and recognition to that which we consider to be of highest worth or value.

But . . . wait a minute. What is "that which we consider to be of highest worth or value"?

God? That's what some people would say. Others might name more than one god or goddess. Still others might say, "We don't believe in

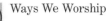

any Supreme Being. But we still follow our own way of worshiping because that's the way we live."

But why is this book called **Ways** *We Worship*? The easiest and clearest way to recognize the differences between one religion and another is what people do about it—the *ways* they live, act, and relate to others because they are followers of a particular religion.

It's sometimes hard to say what a person really believes. Many people may be faithful followers of a certain religion. They may keep all the rules and go to all the worship services. Yet they don't really believe what that religion teaches. They just go along with that way of worshiping—perhaps because it was the religion of their parents and grandparents or perhaps because they like to meet with their friends. For one reason or another, such people still go through the motions of being religious.

This book will try to help you understand what different people believe. But even more than that, this book will try to help you understand what different people *do* because of what they believe—or at least, what they do because of what their friends and fellow worshipers believe.

As you find out more about different religions, you may decide that *Ways We Worship* is a good title for a book like this. Did you know that one of the oldest of all the great religions calls itself *Dao*, meaning "the Way" in Chinese? (See Chapter 6.) Did you know that the biggest of all the world-class religions was already being called "the Way" very early in its history? (See Acts of the Apostles, chapter 9, verse 2, in the Holy Bible; see also Chapter 3 in this book.)

WHAT'S IN THIS BOOK?

What will you find in the next eleven chapters of this book? You'll find a bird's-eye view of most of the world's major religions—a short, clear, honest picture of the different ways different people worship.

Some of the chapters are about only one particular religion. Other chapters group together several religions that are alike in certain ways. Each chapter will help you find answers to important questions such as these:

■ How, when, and where did this religion get started? Who started it? What major historical characters have helped to make it what it is?

■ How has this way of worshiping grown and developed through the centuries? Is it much the same as it used to be, or has it changed a lot? Are all who follow this religion of the same type, or can they be divided into several different types?

■ What is this religion like today? How many followers does it have? Where do they live? Are they growing in numbers? What do they believe, and what do they do because of these beliefs? What influence do they have on the world situation today?

The Number of People in Each of the World's Largest Religions

Roman Catholic Christians	1,058,069,000
Orthodox Christians	174,184,000
Protestant Christians	469,181,000
Other Christians	199,707,000
ALL CHRISTIANS	1,901,141,000
ALL MUSLIMS	1,033,453,000
ALL HINDUS	764,000,000
ALL BUDDHISTS	338,621,000

Source: Encyclopaedia Brittanica Book of the Year, *1995.*

ONE GOD

Why are Chapters 2 through 12 of this book organized into three big sections?

The first section of this book is called "One God." In this section you will find three long chapters about three important religions. Each of these three world religions is greatly different from the other two. Besides that, each of these religions includes within it many different ways of worshiping—so many and so different that some of them seem almost like separate religions in themselves.

As different as these three religions are, followers of all three of them will tell you that they worship only one God. That's why we call them *monotheistic religions*. You already know other words that begin with *mono-*, such as *monorail* and *monopoly;* it shouldn't be too hard for you to guess that a monotheistic religion means a religion with only one God.

Here are several other reasons for putting all three of these ways of worshiping together in the first section of this book:

■ Followers of all three religions read and respect some of the same holy books.

■ Followers of all three religions remember and honor some of the same historical characters.

■ Each of these three great religions has spread into every continent on earth.

■ Each of these three great religions has made a big difference in world history, past and present.

■ Followers of these three great religions now live in more different parts of the globe than followers of any other one religion described in this book.

■ Two of these three great ways of worshiping are the two religions that have the most followers in the world today.

OUT OF ASIA

The second section of this book is called "Out of Asia." It's a strange and fascinating fact that most of the world's major religions have gotten their start in the huge continent of Asia. That's true of the three great monotheistic religions described in Chapters 2 through 4 of this book: all three of them began in the Asian part of the Middle East. It's also true of at least six other major religions, as you can see for yourself in Chapters 5 through 10 of this book.

What is it about Asia that makes it such a fertile field for the planting and growing of religions?

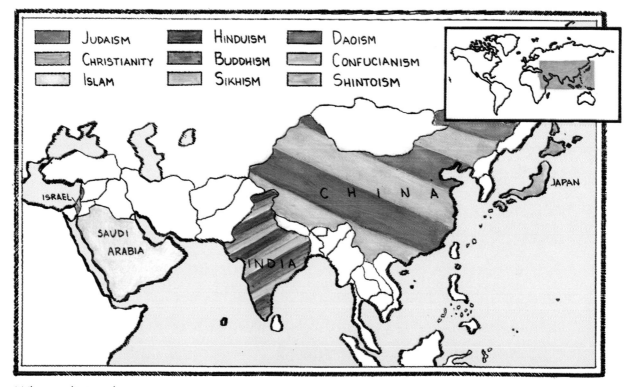

Where religions began.

■ Asia is big. It's by far the largest of all the continents. Asia covers 30 percent of the earth's surface. It stretches from Turkey in the west to Japan in the east and from Siberia in the north to Indonesia in the south.

■ Asia has lots of people. That's where you'll find three of the four largest nations on earth by population: China is number 1, India is number 2, and Indonesia is number 4. (Can you guess which nation is number 3 in world population? It's not located in Asia, but many of its people came from Asia . . . or at least their parents or grandparents did.)

What's the difference between the three out-of-Asia religions in the first section of this book and the six out-of-Asia religions in the second section? You've already read the reasons for grouping three great world religions together in one section. What's so different about those other major religions in the second section?

For one thing, the six religions in the second section of this book haven't spread out of Asia as quickly or as widely as the three religions in the first section. Yes, you may find followers of these out-of-Asia religions among your friends and neighbors—but probably not a lot of them.

Most people still think of these ways of worshiping as being mainly Asian religions, even though some of them have in fact moved out into other continents as well. So, should we call them "world" religions, or not? What do you think?

IN EVERY CONTINENT

The last section of this book is called "In Every Continent." Besides all of the great religions described in the first two sections of this book, there are also many other ways of worshiping. Some of these religions got their start in particular places, such as in Africa, the Americas, or Australasia.

Others have appeared in different forms at different times and places, yet they seem much alike in certain ways.

Why are all these many different religions described in only two chapters in the third section of this book? Aren't the religions grouped together in Chapters 11 and 12 just as important as the ways of worshiping described in more detail in Chapters 2 through 10?

Yes, of course, all ways of worshiping are important, because all of them grow out of the honor and recognition we give to that which we consider to be of highest worth or value. Yes, of course, every religion is important to followers of that religion.

But . . . do you have any idea how many different religions there are in the world today? Nobody knows for sure, but the number surely goes into the thousands. In Japan alone some people say there are as many as *one hundred new religions started every year.*

It would take an enormous encyclopedia to give a separate chapter telling in detail about every known religion. That's why choices had to be made in organizing and preparing this book.

The first two sections of this book tell briefly about nine major religions. Each of these ways of worshiping has already lasted for hundreds or even thousands of years. Each of them is still being followed today by many millions of the people of our world.

The third section of this book tells about many other religions. These other religions are all lumped together in that final section for one or more of the following reasons:

■ These other ways of worshiping have fewer followers than the great religions described in Chapters 2 through 10.

■ These ways of worshiping were mainly followed in the past, not in the present.

■ These ways of worshiping got started much later in human history than the great religions described in Chapters 2 through 10.

■ These ways of worshiping are mainly followed today only in certain countries or areas, not in the whole world.

DIFFERENT PEOPLE, DIFFERENT IDEAS

Some people may not agree with the way religions have been sorted out into sections and chapters in this book. For instance:

■ Followers of the Sikh religion (see Chapter 10) might say that their way of worshiping should have been included in the section "One God."

■ Latter-Day Saints (Mormons), Jehovah's Witnesses, or members of the Unification Church (followers of Sun Myung Moon) might say that their religions should have been included in Chapter 3, "The Way of the Christ," instead of being put in Chapter 12.

■ Certain Catholic Christians and certain Protestant Christians (see Chapter 3) might say that people outside their particular groups are not really followers of Jesus the Christ at all.

■ Some Chinese people might say that they are Daoists (see Chapter 6), Buddhists (see Chapter 8), and Confucianists (see Chapter 9) all at the same time, without seeing any contradiction in this.

Please remember: This book is not intended to show that any particular religion is good or bad, right or wrong. It is intended to give you a quick look at many different ways people worship. In order to do that, some choices had to be made: How many chapters and sections should be included in the book? Which ways of worshiping should be put into which of those chapters and sections?

Different people have different ways of deciding who is a follower of a certain religion and who isn't. For example, read about several people who may be near your own age:

Sofie

■ Sofie lives in Austria. Like many other Austrians, Sofie and her whole family will tell you that they are Christians of the Roman Catholic type (see Chapter 3). Yet they never attend *mass*, or the main Roman Catholic worship service, even though services are held every Sunday at the church just down the street from their house. Would you say Sofie is or isn't a Christian?

Budi

■ Budi lives in Indonesia. Like many other Indonesians, Budi and his whole family will tell you that they are Muslims (or Moslems) of the

Sunnite type (see Chapter 4). Yet they never go to Muslim worship services, even though these are held every Friday at the masjid (or mosque) just down the street from their house. Would you say Budi is or isn't a Muslim?

■ Jamal lives in New York. He and his family are followers of The Nation of Islam. They will tell you that they are true Muslims. But many Muslims in other countries do not agree; they say that The Nation of Islam in the United States is not really an Islamic way of worshiping. What do you think?

■ Kim and Walker both live in California. Kim thinks all religions all over the world are basically the same. Walker strongly disagrees with this idea. What do you think?

Different people also have different ideas about when their ways of worshiping got started. For example, take Abraham, who lived in the Asian part of the Middle East about four thousand years ago. (See the timeline at the back of the book.)

 ■ Followers of the way of Judaism (see Chapter 2) honor Abraham as one of the founding fathers of their religion. Because of this, they say that their way of worshiping got started thousands of years ago.

■ Christians (see Chapter 3) agree that Abraham was one of the founders of Judaism, but they also honor Abraham as one of many people in ancient times who looked forward to the coming of the Christ. The Christian way of worshiping got started only about

two thousand years ago (see the timeline again); yet Christians believe their religious roots go back much farther than that in human history.

■ Muslims (see Chapter 4) believe that Abraham was really a follower of the way of Islam, because he submitted to the will of God—which is what it means to be a Muslim. Because of this Muslims don't like to say that their way of worshiping got started with the Prophet Muhammad in the seventh century A.D. (see the timeline); they believe it goes back much earlier than that, even back to the creation of the universe.

Many worshipers believe that their own religion goes back to the beginning of all things. But this book mainly tries to show *ways* people worship—what people *do* because they believe certain things. Because of that, this book doesn't tell much about ancient times, about the distant shadowy past before there were any written records. Instead, this book begins the story of each religion at the time when that way of worshiping clearly shows up in human history. For Christianity (Chapter 3), that means the story begins about two thousand years ago. For Islam (Chapter 4), that means the story begins in the seventh century A.D.

READ ON AND FIND ANSWERS!

As you read this book, it may bother you to learn about things you don't agree with. You may wonder how in the world some people's ways of worshiping ever got started. You may think the sections and chapters in this book are all wrong in the way they've been put together.

Never mind; read the book anyway. Maybe you'll learn something interesting. Maybe you'll find out why some things are important to you and why other things aren't. Maybe you'll begin to see why the things that mean the most to you may not be the same things that mean the most to some of your friends and neighbors.

Remember: *Ways We Worship* may or may not be the best title for this book. A true believer would say that religion influences every part of his or her life, not just certain parts of it labeled as worship.

But the book had to have some kind of title, didn't it? After you've read all twelve chapters, maybe you'll agree that whether we recognize it or not, the ways we worship can play a big part in making all of us who we are.

Part 1

One God

2 The Way of Judaism

Rebekah's seat was empty when attendance was checked that morning. So was Aaron's. "Hey, where are those guys?" Tara wondered aloud.

Ms. Blake explained, "Today is a holiday on their calendar."

Tara blinked. "How come the rest of us don't get a holiday, too?"

"Because the rest of us don't worship in the same way Aaron and Rebekah and their families do."

"You mean . . . they have a different calendar, just because they have a different religion?" Tara asked. "Cool!"

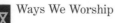

WHO ARE THEY?

Perhaps, like Tara, you have friends at school or in your neighborhood who follow the way of Judaism. Perhaps, like Aaron or Rebekah, you're Jewish yourself. You may already know that followers of Judaism place great importance on holidays and holy days.

Who are these people who observe so many holidays and holy days?

A Calendar of Jewish Holidays and Holy Days

Purim: In February or March (see page 31).

Passover: In March or April (see pages 26–28).

Shavuot: Seven weeks after Passover (see page 29).

Rosh Hashanah: In September or October (see page 24).

Yom Kippur: Ten days after Rosh Hashanah (see page 24–25).

Sukkot: Five days after Yom Kippur (see page 28).

Simchat Torah: Nine days after Sukkot (see page 28).

Hanukkah/Chanukah: In late November or December (see pages 31 and 32).

Can you recognize a Jewish person by the way he or she looks?

No, generally not. Jews are white and black, tall and short, darkhaired and blond. In Brazil there are hundreds of Chinese Jews whose ancestors came from East Asia. In Israel there are thousands of black Jews whose ancestors came from Ethiopia . . . and also from the south side of Chicago!

Can you recognize a Jewish person by his or her name?

No, generally not. For instance, take the names used in conversations at the beginnings of the first two chapters in this book: Aaron and

Rebekah (or Rebecca) are names used by Jews and non-Jews alike.

Surely you can recognize a Jewish person by the way he or she worships, can't you?

Not necessarily. Some Jews observe every holiday and holy day of Judaism, whether it comes once a week or once a year. Others never do anything outwardly that shows their religion; yet if you asked them, they would be quick to tell you they are Jewish.

How can you find out, then, who really is Jewish and who isn't?

Jewish people themselves disagree about the right answer to that one. They have argued about it a lot, especially in Israel, for Israel is the one country in the world that has a very special relationship to Judaism.

Some people will give you this answer to the question: *A Jew is anyone who says he or she is Jewish.* Other people will tell you that this definition is much too broad. Why?

Basically, there are two ways of becoming Jewish:

1. Be born to a Jewish mother.
2. Decide on your own that you want to start worshiping according to the way of Judaism, and then follow through on your decision.
   (*Convert* is a word often used for someone who decides to join a particular worshiping community.)

Are you still Jewish if you are born to a Jewish mother, yet you later choose to follow some other way of worshiping?

That depends. Most Jews would say you stop being Jewish if (for instance) you become a Christian. But some Christians born of a Jewish mother say they are just as Jewish as ever. "After all," they remind us, "Jesus himself was a Jew."

Judaism is much older than Christianity or Islam, the other two great religions described in the first section of this book. In fact, it is one of the oldest of all world religions and is still going strong today.

Judaism has far fewer followers than the other two great religions included in this section. In fact, it is the smallest religious group that has a separate chapter in this book. Yet Judaism has had more influence on the history of the world than almost any other religion.

How, when, and where did the way of Judaism get started?

Let's answer that question in an unusual way. Remember what you read a moment ago: Holidays and holy days are extremely important in Judaism. Let's look at some Jewish festivals of worship, whether held once a week or once a year. For as we do that, we'll be acting out a retelling of the long history of Judaism.

Names—Ancient and Modern

Jew: Anyone who was born of a Jewish mother (or who chooses to follow the Jewish way of worshiping).

Judaism: The religion of the Jews. Both Judaism and Jew come from the name of Judah, one of the founding fathers of the Jewish people.

Hebrew: Another name for the Jewish people in ancient times. Hebrew is also the name of the ancient language they spoke. This language has since developed into modern Hebrew, spoken in Israel today.

Israelite: Another name for the Jewish people in ancient times.

Israeli: A citizen of the modern country of Israel, founded in 1948. Both Israelite and Israeli come from the name of Israel (also called Jacob), one of the founding fathers of the Jewish people.

FROM THE CREATION

Followers of Judaism like to worship every day of the week, but their day of rest, when the main worship services are held, always falls on a Saturday—or on the *Sabbath* day. Why Saturday? Because Jews read in the very first chapter of their very first holy book that God Almighty created the heavens and the earth in six days, and then rested on the seventh day. Since Sunday (not Monday) is the first day of the week, then Saturday is the seventh day. The word *Sabbath* comes from the Hebrew word for resting.

Following ancient tradition, Jewish people count their weekly Sabbath from sundown Friday till sundown Saturday. For many of them, the highlight of each Sabbath is the Friday evening meal, eaten at home with the family. They light special candles—sometimes only two, sometimes one for each member of the family. They eat *hallah* (or *challah*), bread baked in braided loaves. They offer special prayers of blessing.

A Passover meal (see pp. 26–28.)

For other Jews, it's just as important to gather at their place of worship on the Sabbath day, whether Friday night or Saturday morning or Saturday afternoon—or all three. The *cantor* (music leader) sings or chants special hymns. The holy scroll-books are carefully taken out of their special storage place. The *rabbi* (a teacher, spiritual leader, and counselor) or some other worshiper reads solemn words written by ancient lawgivers and prophets.

THE NEW YEAR

Just as the Sabbath becomes the most important time in the week for Jewish worshipers, so the high holy days become the most important time in the year. The Jewish new year comes not in January but in September or October. The exact date isn't always the same because Judaism follows a lunar calendar, based on when the new moon shows up in the sky.

Rosh Hashanah means head of the year in Hebrew. Only at this time once a year can you hear in Jewish worship services the blowing of the *shofar*—a curved trumpet made of a ram's horn. In olden times these special trumpets were sometimes blasted to honor Hebrew kings. Nowadays, the only king honored by their piercing sound is God Almighty, King of the universe.

Rosh Hashanah is only the beginning of the Jewish new year festival. Ten days later comes *Yom Kippur*, or Day of Atonement. Our custom of making new year's resolutions probably comes from the Jewish tradition of saying once a year, "I'm sorry and ashamed of everything I did wrong last year. With God's help, I'll do better next year." That's where the word *atonement* comes from, for this confession and promise helps the worshiper feel *at-one* with God, not separated from God by sin and guilt.

In ancient days, Yom Kippur was one of many times when the Jewish people would bring a cow or sheep or goat (or even two pigeons if they couldn't afford anything bigger) to be sacrificed to God on an altar.

Yom Kippur also reminds Jewish worshipers of one very special time of sacrifice in the early history of their religion. They count a man named Abraham as one of the *patriarchs*, or founding fathers of their way of worshiping. About four thousand years ago, Abraham lived in the land of great rivers now called Iraq. There he turned away from the worship of many gods. Following special directions from the one Lord God, Abraham set out across the desert to the land now called Israel, Palestine, and Jordan.

For many years Abraham and his wife Sarah had no children. Then God promised them a son. The promised son was born at last and was given the name Isaac. When Isaac had grown to perhaps about the age you are now, Abraham felt that God was directing him to make the most

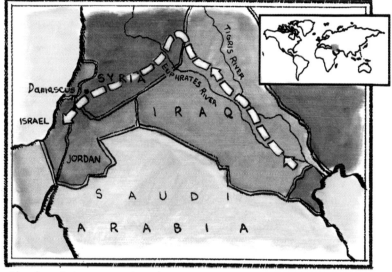

Abraham's journey to Israel.

terrible of all sacrifices. Like the idol-worshipers who lived all around him, Abraham got ready to kill his only son on the altar.

At the last minute, God told Abraham that the idea of sacrificing Isaac was only a test to see whether he would really follow all of God's commands. Instead of a son, God directed that a sheep should be laid on the altar of sacrifice. Around the site of Abraham's altar, the Jewish people in later years built the city of Jerusalem, with its great Temple for worshiping the one Lord God.

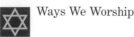

FROM SLAVERY TO FREEDOM

So Abraham's son Isaac lived to grow up. He and his wife Rebekah had twin sons, Esau and Jacob (later called Israel). Jacob later had a total of twelve sons, and they in turn became the founding fathers of the twelve tribes of Israel.

Some of the most interesting stories in all of world literature tell us what happened to these sons of Israel: Reuben and Simeon, Judah and Levi, Joseph and Benjamin, and all the rest. You can read these stories for yourself in Genesis, the first part of the Jewish Scriptures known as "Torah."

By a strange turn of events, the great-grandchildren of the sons of Israel found themselves slaves in the land of Egypt. After many years of hardship, God sent a man named Moses to lead them out of slavery. When the king of Egypt refused to let them go, God caused all kinds of disasters (known as the ten plagues), including epidemics, hailstorms, polluted rivers, crop failures, and swarms of gnats, flies, and grasshoppers. The worst of all these disasters came one dreadful night when the firstborn son in each Egyptian household died. The Egyptians' Hebrew slaves had been warned in advance to make special preparations, and the angel of death passed over all the Hebrew houses.

With the help of his sister, Miriam, and his brother, Aaron, Moses led the Israelites to break out of slavery. But then the Egyptian army tracked them down to the water's edge. There Moses raised his staff, and the waters parted so the Hebrews could cross safely to the other side. When the slavemasters tried to chase them, the waters closed again and drowned the entire Egyptian army.

This tremendous event is what Jewish worshipers celebrate in the spring of every year, at the time of the *Passover*. (Remember how the angel of death passed over the Hebrew houses?) Each type of food eaten at that holy festival has a special meaning:

■ The bread is flat and thin, because the Israelites left Egypt in too much of a hurry to mix yeast with their dough.

■ The main dish is roasted meat; some Jews eat roasted lamb because the Hebrews were told to mark lamb's blood on their doorposts so the angel of death would see it and pass them by.

■ Bitter herbs, usually horseradish, remind the Jewish people what a hard time their ancestors had as slaves in Egypt.

■ A paste mixed of chopped apples, walnuts or almonds, cinnamon, and wine or grapejuice is a reminder of the mortar the Israelites used in making bricks during their time of slavery.

■ The Cup of Elijah, a special cup of wine, is an important symbol of welcome for the prophet Elijah, who the Jews believe visits every Jewish home during the Passover meal and blesses it. The invisible guest brings good cheer into Jewish homes on all happy occasions, especially on the first night of Passover.

Moses raised his staff and the waters parted.

The youngest member of each Jewish family gets to play a special part at Passover time. The child asks a list of important questions, starting with, "Why is this night different from all other nights?" Answers to the questions tell the child and everybody else about that great event in Hebrew history which the Passover feast reminds them of.

THE LAW OF MOSES

After Moses led the Israelites out of slavery in Egypt, they lived for a long time as nomads, wandering in the desert. Jewish worshipers of today remember that part of their history, too. Once a year they build tent like shelters of leaves and branches, and live under these for a little while. This is called *Sukkot*, or the festival of Shelters.

During that time in the desert, Moses led the people to make a *covenant*, or special promise, with the Lord God himself. Moses told the Hebrews what God said they must do and not do, if they were to become God's special people. The first and greatest of these rules and regulations were the Ten Commandments. Many people of today—Jews and non-Jews alike—think these ten great guidelines are the most important laws for living ever made.

As you might expect, Jewish people also have a holy day to help them remember the Law of Moses. In their weekly worship services during each year, they read through the entire *Torah*, or five books of the Law. These books are Genesis, Exodus, Leviticus, Numbers, and Deuteronomy —the first five parts of the Jewish Scriptures. Jewish people celebrate their annual festival of *Simchat Torah* in the worship service when they finish reading the last verses of Deuteronomy and start all over again with the first verses of Genesis. It's a happy time, a time for parades and banners, for apples and nuts and cakes. On the Jewish calendar, it comes in the fall, after the festival of Shelters (or Sukkot).

The Ten Commandments

1. I the Lord am your God...: You shall have no other gods besides Me.
2. You shall not make for yourself a sculptured image.... You shall not bow down to them or serve them.
3. You shall not swear falsely by the name of the Lord your God.
4. Remember the sabbath day and keep it holy.
5. Honor your father and your mother.
6. You shall not murder.
7. You shall not commit adultery.
8. You shall not steal.
9. You shall not bear false witness against your neighbor.
10. You shall not covet... anything that is your neighbors.

Tanakh; The Holy Scriptures. Copyright © 1985 by the Jewish Publication Society. Exodus 20:2–5, 7–8, 12–14.

Another joyous holiday comes in late spring or early summer, seven weeks after the Passover. It's called *Shavuot,* or the festival of Weeks, because it comes seven Sabbaths (or seven weeks) after Passover. In olden times when many Hebrews were farmers, they kept the festival of Weeks as a spring harvest celebration—much like Americans observing Thanksgiving Day.

Today, as Shavuot time rolls around again, Jewish worshipers remember the time when God gave Moses the Ten Commandments. Also, Jewish boys and girls often hear again one of the oldest and loveliest stories ever written: the beautiful story of Ruth, who worked in a harvest field and there found happiness and a new home among the Jewish people. You can read the story of Ruth for yourself in the Jewish Scriptures.

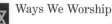

GOOD TIMES AND BAD

Not all of the holidays and holy days of Judaism look back to happy times in Hebrew history.

Long after the days of Abraham and Joseph and Moses, the Hebrews were ruled by judges like Gideon, Deborah, Samson, Samuel, and several more. Still later, they were ruled by kings. The greatest of the kings was David, Ruth's great-grandson, born a shepherd boy. David was also the greatest writer of Psalms, the ancient Hebrew songs of praise.

David is still fondly remembered today by a six-pointed star, the *Mogen David* or Shield of David. Often you will see this symbol of Judaism—in pictures, on books, on places of worship.

A Psalm of David

The Lord is my shepherd; I lack nothing.
He makes me lie down in green pastures;
He leads me to water in places of repose;
He renews my life;
He guides me in right paths as befits His name.
Though I walk through a valley of deepest darkness,
I fear no harm, Lord, for You are with me;
Your rod and Your staff—they comfort me.
You spread a table for me in full view of my enemies;
You anoint my head with oil; my drink is abundant.
Only goodness and steadfast love shall pursue me
all the days of my life,
and I shall dwell in the house of the Lord for many long years.

Tanakh; The Holy Scriptures. Copyright © 1985 by the Jewish Publication Society. Psalms 23:1-6

Not all of those who led the Jewish people in ancient times were great like King David, wise like King Solomon, good like King Josiah, or even brave though wicked like King Ahab. The people of Israel broke up into warring clans. Often they forgot the Lord God and worshiped the same idols their neighbors did. Finally they were carried off into slavery again—this time, in the land of great rivers where their fore-father Abraham had gotten his start so many centuries before. Other Jews scattered to other places.

The Book of Esther in the Jewish Scriptures tells of a time when an evil man plotted to wipe out all the Jews in Persia (or Iran as we call it today). But brave Queen Esther, a descendant of the tribe of Benjamin, managed to foil his plot.

Jewish boys and girls help act out this exciting story all over again in February or March of every year, at the time of the feast of *Purim*. In Esther chapter 3, verse 7, and chapter 9, verses 26–28, you can read how the festival gets its name: Purim means a way of drawing straws, which was what the Jews' enemy did when he was trying to decide the best time to destroy them.

Throughout history there have been people who have tried to wipe out the Jews. Why? One reason may be because Jewish people have always stood up for important things, even if that made them seem different from everybody else. When everybody else worshiped many idol-gods, Jews worshiped the one Lord God. When everybody else was acting wild and wicked, Jews kept their lives clean and their outlook straight.

A little over two thousand years ago, it was the Syrians' turn to try to destroy the Jewish way of life. But a brave family of brothers fought back against the mighty Syrian army with its battle-trained elephants. They led their people to freedom. When they drove the enemy out of

Jerusalem, they found that the Temple, the great central place for Jewish worship, had been left littered with filth. They cleaned it up and rededicated the altar, celebrating for eight days. The Jewish people believe that the brothers found a small amount of oil, enough to last one day—but it lasted eight days! Jews today celebrate this occasion by lighting candles on a *menorah* for eight nights.

This event is joyfully celebrated near the end of each year. Those who worship according to the way of Judaism call it *Hanukkah* (*Chanukah*), or the festival of Lights, or the feast of Dedication. Jewish people remember with songs and dances and gifts and games how the great Temple in Jerusalem was rededicated to God, after enemies had made such a mess of it. And the menorah, with its many lights, has become another symbol for modern Judaism, along with the star of David.

ANTI-SEMITISM

How good it would be if we could say that plots to wipe out the Jews only happened long ago and far away! The sad truth is that *anti-Semitism* (anti-Jewish feelings and actions) has continued throughout the centuries and has spread all over the world.

A turning point in the long history of Judaism came with the founding of Christianity. Jesus the Christ, its founder, was a Jew, as were nearly all of his first followers. But little by little, more non-Jews than Jews became

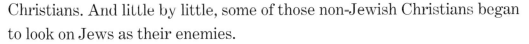

Christians. And little by little, some of those non-Jewish Christians began to look on Jews as their enemies.

During the Middle Ages, most of Europe was ruled by Christians; most of the Middle East and North Africa was ruled by Muslims. Followers of both religions gave Jewish people a hard time, but Christians were even harder on them than Muslims were.

At first, certain Christians of Europe began to say to their Jewish neighbors, "You may not live among us as Jews." They passed all kinds of laws making life hard for Jewish people. The laws didn't apply to Jews who chose to become Christians.

In later centuries, certain Christians of Europe looked at their Jewish neighbors and decided, "You may not live among us, period." That marked the beginning of the *ghetto*, or section of each city set aside for Jews.

Still later, certain Christians (mainly in Russia and eastern Europe) looked at the Jews living in the ghetto and decided, "You may not live, period." That marked the beginning of the *pogrom*, or campaign to wipe out all Jewish people in a certain area.

Did things get better through the centuries, as people of Europe came out of the Middle Ages and made progress in many ways?

Yes and no. The Jews of Europe themselves blossomed as never before. Few people realize how many of the world's greatest writers, musicians, scientists, and thinkers have been Jews. From the music of Itzhak Perlman and Leonard Bernstein to the theories of Sigmund Freud and Albert Einstein, Jewish people have left their mark on the modern world.

But all of that meant nothing when an evil man named Adolf Hitler began to rule Germany in the 1930s. Hitler led the worst campaign of anti-Semitism in all of human history. Between 1933 and 1945, he and his followers wiped out one third of all the Jews on earth—six million men, women, and children. If you have read such books as *The Diary of a Young Girl* by Anne Frank or seen such films as *Schindler's List,* then you know at least a little about what a horrible time that was—especially for Jewish people in Europe. No wonder this time is often called the *Holocaust,* a word that means complete destruction.

This most terrible of all pogroms helped speed up a plan that certain Jews and non-Jews had been working together on for many years. Their plan was to start a new country in the region where Abraham and Isaac had lived so long ago: Palestine. "If people in other countries don't want Jews," these planners said, "then let's make a place where all Jewish people will be welcomed."

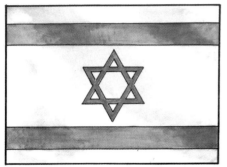

Flag of Israel.

That was how the modern country of Israel got its start, in 1948. The land of Palestine was divided up to make a new country. Millions of Jews from all over the world moved back to the ancient homeland of their forefathers.

Not all Israelis are Jews, however. Some are Muslims; some are Christians; some do not follow any religion. Even half a century after the founding of Israel, arguments and fights between Israelis and their non-Jewish neighbors are still making newspaper headlines in the Middle East.

DIVISIONS IN JUDAISM

Even after Hitler tried to wipe out all the Jews of Europe, there are still at least thirteen million Jewish people living in the world today. About one third of them live in Israel. More than a third of them live in the United States—two million in New York City alone. The rest are scattered all over the globe. (Of course, not all of these people actually worship according to the way of Judaism; remember how hard it is to say who really is Jewish and who isn't?)

Most American Jews fit into one of three main types: Orthodox, Reform, or Conservative.

- *Orthodox Jews* try to keep their lives as close as possible to the way their ancestors lived in ancient times. They eat no pork or shellfish, because these foods were not a part of the menu given by the Law of Moses. They do no work on the Sabbath. They call their house of worship a *synagogue* (a word that means assembly hall) just like the Jews of twenty centuries ago. Women and girls worship separately from men and boys. Some Orthodox Jews even follow strict religious tradition by wearing special clothes and wearing their hair in special ways.

- *Reform Jews* try to adapt their ancient religion to modern life. They think that Jerusalem is not the only place for a Temple; instead, they call each local place of worship a temple. They no longer observe every single rule about food and drink, about what to wear and when to worship. They read their ancient holy books in English as well as in Hebrew, so more people can understand. They encourage women and girls to become as much involved in worship as men and boys. Reform Jews feel that these changes have made their old way of worshiping stronger and more effective.

- *Conservative Jews* try to find and follow the middle of the road. They say, "Let's *conserve* all that's good about the old ways, without becoming as strict and stiff as Orthodox Jews are. Let's also *conserve* some of the ways Reform Jews have adapted our faith to the modern world. Let's *conserve* our oneness as Jews, whatever differences we may have. Above all, let's *conserve* the things that are most important to us, especially our sacred Law."

JOINING THE WORSHIPING COMMUNITY

A big event for many Jewish boys and girls comes in their early teens. It got started with the old custom of *bar mitzvah*, or son of the covenant.

On his thirteenth birthday, or the Sabbath day nearest to it, a Jewish boy will strap two small black boxes onto his body—one on his forehead, one on his left arm. Inside each little box is an important quotation from the books of Exodus and Deuteronomy in the Jewish Scriptures; Moses himself told his people to follow such a custom.

Besides the boxes filled with scripture verses, the boy will also put on a small round cap (called a yarmulka) and will drape over his shoulders a shawl with fringes. In the Jewish place of worship, he will stand up and read from the *Torah*, the scroll-book in which the Law of Moses is written. This is a sign that he is now old enough to become a son of the covenant, a full member of the Jewish group of worshipers, and to take on responsibility for his own conduct.

Some Jews keep bar mitzvah as a special privilege for boys only. Other Jews think girls shouldn't be left out, and so they also observe the ceremony of *bat mitzvah*, or daughter of the covenant. Other Jewish worshipers also hold another special ceremony when both girls and boys are about fifteen called *confirmation*, to make these young worshipers *firm* in the Jewish faith into which they were born.

Bar mitzvah

JUDAISM WORLDWIDE

Throughout the centuries, Jewish people have become great travelers. Sometimes they have moved by choice; sometimes other people have forced them to move. Wherever you live, Jewish people may well be living nearby.

Maybe reading this chapter has helped you understand why anti-Semitism is so ugly. It doesn't always take such horrible forms as it did during the Hitler years. Sometimes it crops up in telling certain jokes, calling people names, or scrawling signs on places of worship.

Remember! From the time of Moses till now, the way of Judaism has emphasized these two most important beliefs:

■ God is one, and we should love God with all there is of us.

■ We should also love our neighbors—*all* of our neighbors—as much as we love ourselves.

Milestones Along the Way of Judaism

Being born: When a Jewish baby boy is eight days old, he is *circumcised*; the foreskin of his penis is removed. At the same time the boy is named. Both boy and girl babies are taken to the house of worship, where their names are announced.

Joining the worshiping community: On page 36 you can read about *bar mitzvah, bat mitzvah,* and confirmation.

Getting married: The bride and groom stand under a canopy and share a glass of wine. At the end of the ceremony, the groom breaks a glass under his foot; this is a reminder that the Temple in Jerusalem has been destroyed and that all of life is touched with sadness as well as joy.

Dying: A dead body is buried quickly, within two days. People who have lost someone they love are encouraged to cry and show their grief. Mourners recite a special prayer of remembrance—not just at the funeral, but also once a week or even once a day for the next year.

3 The Way of the Christ

On Sunday mornings, Tara rides with her dad to a modern building that sprawls on three sides of a big parking lot. She hurries into a special once-a-week class with others her own age; their textbook is the Holy Bible. After class, Tara walks into a long, high-ceilinged auditorium and sits down on a cushioned bench. She hears the soft tones of an organ and joins in singing hymns printed in a thick book. She listens to readings from the Holy Bible and to a sermon explaining those readings.

Tara is worshiping according to the way of the Christ.

On Saturday nights, Kevin rides with his mother to a rented school building. There are plenty of folding chairs, but the people who have gathered for worship don't seem to use them much. More often they're standing up as they sing words of praise projected onto a big screen. Kevin claps as he sings; so does his mother. Some of his friends raise their hands high; some look up with closed eyes; some kneel on the carpet or even stretch out full length as the singing goes on.

Kevin is worshiping according to the way of the Christ.

Eileen gets up early on Sundays and walks to an old-fashioned brick building with spires pointing toward the sky. As she enters the dimly lit auditorium, she dips her fingers into a small container of water near the back wall, bows quickly, and makes signs in front of her face and chest. Smoke from candles and sweet-smelling incense swirl in the early-morning sunlight that filters through high windows of colored glass. Men and boys in long robes move quietly near the front—sometimes facing the worshipers, sometimes turning away from them. Again and again Eileen kneels, stands up, sits down, and then kneels once more.

Eileen is worshiping according to the way of the Christ.

Raygene goes to worship in a small building that used to be a store. Women dressed in white, even down to white gloves, usher Raygene to a seat—and, later on, march up and down several times to collect offerings of money from the worshipers. The singing might sound more like shouting to someone who wasn't used to Raygene's church. Everybody takes part; even when the pastor starts preaching, people often punctuate his sermon with cries of "Amen!" and "That's right!" and "Bless the Lord!"

Raygene is worshiping according to the way of the Christ.

On a weekday evening after school, John slips quietly into his neighbor's house. Doors are closed and window-blinds are drawn, so outsiders can't see who's there and what they're doing. John listens closely to readings from the Holy Bible, because he doesn't have a copy of his own to read at home. In fact, "John" is only the name he uses with others who worship as he does: Outside, he has another name, for in John's country it's against the law to follow John's religion.

John is worshiping according to the way of the Christ.

Holy Books of Three Religions

The Holy Bible: A book of holy books, all or a part of which are read and respected by worshipers who follow the way of Judaism, the way of the Christ, and the way of Islam.

Testament: The same as *covenant*, or special promise between God and God's people.

Old Testament: The first main section of the Holy Bible; its 39 books include the Law of Moses and the early history of the Jews as God's special people. This "old covenant" is the only part of the Holy Bible used by Jewish worshipers today.

New Testament: The second and last main section of the Holy Bible; its 27 books tell the story of Jesus and his first followers. This "new covenant" explains that God's special promise is now available to anyone who believes in Jesus Christ.

WHAT IS CHRISTIANITY?

How can all these different ways of worshiping be called the same thing? What is the way of the Christ? Or, to give it a more common name, what is *Christianity*?

In the first place, you need to learn something many people don't know: *Christ* is not a name. It's really a title, and it means the same thing as *Messiah*: "the Anointed One." When a king was crowned in olden times, oil or ointment was placed on his forehead to show how special he was. In other words, he was "*an-ointed.*" (So was Queen Elizabeth II, at her coronation in 1953 as Great Britain's head of state.)

Through the long history of the Jewish people, many prophets predicted, "Someday God will send a great King, an *Anointed One* (or Christ or Messiah)." Christians believe that these prophecies came true in the life of a Jewish man known in his own time and place as Jesus of Nazareth. That's why Christians call him Jesus *the Christ*, or Jesus Christ for short.

How long ago did Jesus live? That's easy; what year is it now? Most people all over the world, Christians and non-Christians alike, count years from the birth of Jesus. The abbreviation B.C. stands for Before Christ. A.D. stands for the Latin words *Anno Domini*, meaning Year of Our Lord. (Some people prefer to use B.C.E., Before the Common Era, and C.E., Common Era.) So even the calendar on the wall will tell you it was about two thousand years ago when a Jewish boy was born in Palestine and given the name Jesus.

Special Names and Titles for Jesus

Christ: A title meaning "the Anointed One"—the great King whom God promised to send.

Messiah: A title meaning the same as *Christ*. (Have you ever listened to music from Handel's *Messiah*, at Christmas or Easter time?)

Jesus: Human name of the person believed to be the Anointed One, or the great King sent by God. (Jesus in Greek is the same as Joshua in Hebrew; both names mean Savior, or God saves.)

You can read prophecies about the Christ in the Old Testament, the first big section of the Holy Bible. People who worship according to the way of Judaism (see Chapter 2 of this book) believe that this is all there is of the Scriptures. But Christians believe that the Bible also includes the New Testament, which tells about the coming of Christ.

According to the New Testament, the birth of Jesus was a *miracle*—something that cannot be explained by natural processes. His mother, *Mary of Nazareth*, had never had a sexual partner; this is why Christians call her the *Virgin Mary*. Christians believe that when Jesus was born to Mary in Bethlehem, angel messengers and a blazing star told how special he was.

Special Days for Christians

Christmas: Traditional date for celebrating the birth of Jesus the Christ, or his *Nativity*; no one really knows the exact day, or even the time of year.
Good Friday: Day for remembering Jesus' death on the cross, or his *crucifixion*. This date is more accurate than the date for Jesus' birth; the records agree that Jesus did indeed die on a Friday in springtime.
Easter: Sunday celebrating the morning in springtime when Jesus arose from death. Most Christians celebrate this *resurrection* by meeting for worship on Sunday (also called the Sabbath or the Lord's Day) rather than on Saturday, the Jewish Sabbath.

When Jesus had grown to the age of about thirty, he left his family home in the village of Nazareth and began to wander around the little land of Palestine, showing and telling people how they could know God better. He taught that God is our loving Father. He healed many who were sick.

He made cripples walk, caused the blind to see, and even raised the dead at least three different times. He also stopped a storm on the Sea of Galilee and made a little boy's picnic lunch into enough food for five thousand hungry people, with several basketfuls left over. No wonder great crowds followed the teacher from Nazareth!

Among those crowds were men and women who became Jesus' closest followers. A list of their names might sound like a class roll at your school today: Peter, Andrew, Mary, Martha, James, John, Susanna, Joanna, Matthew, Simon, Thomas, and Philip.

These men and women listened in awe to the teachings of Jesus—teachings now known and loved all over the world. Many of them were in the form of stories (or *parables*: The Lost Sheep, The Good Samaritan, and The Prodigal Son, just to name a few).

But not everyone agreed with what Jesus was doing. Religious leaders thought he was telling people that rules weren't too important, as long as you loved God and loved your neighbor, too. Kings and governors feared he would stir up the common people and start a revolution.

Teachings of Jesus

Jesus' disciples gathered around him, and he taught them:
God blesses those people who depend only on him.
They belong to the kingdom of heaven!
God blesses those people who grieve.
They will find comfort!
God blesses those people who are humble.
The earth will belong to them!
God blesses those people who want to obey him
more than to eat or drink.
They will be given what they want!
God blesses those people who are merciful.
They will be treated with mercy!
God blesses those people whose hearts are pure.
They will see him!
God blesses those people who make peace.
They will be called his children!
God blesses those people who are treated badly for doing right.
They belong to the kingdom of heaven.

The Holy Bible: Contemporary English Version, Copyright © 1995, American Bible Society.
Matthew 5:1–10, quoted with permission.

Finally one night Jesus' enemies caught up with him. They whipped him till his back was bloody. Then they nailed him to two crossed pieces of wood; this horrible torture, called *crucifixion*, was the usual way of executing common criminals in that time and place. After hours of agony, Jesus died on the cross. He was buried in a cave-like tomb.

But on the Sunday morning after Jesus had died on Friday, his followers began to report that they had seen him alive again! Over the

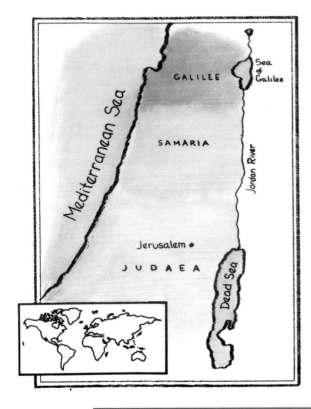

next six weeks, hundreds of people saw the living Jesus—beside the Sea of Galilee, on a mountaintop, walking along a dusty road near Jerusalem, and even inside a locked upstairs room. Many of these same people also saw Jesus when he left this earth. His going was as much a miracle as his coming, for he rose up into the sky and disappeared into the clouds. He told his followers that he would come back again someday, as Judge and King.

More Teachings of Jesus

Pray then like this:
Our Father who art in heaven,
Hallowed be thy name.
Thy kingdom come,
Thy will be done,
On earth as it is in heaven.
Give us this day our daily bread;
And forgive us our debts
As we also have forgiven our debtors.
And lead us not into temptation
But deliver us from evil.

*God loved the people of this world so much
that he gave his only Son,
so that everyone who has faith in him
will have eternal life and never really die.
I am the way, the truth, and the life!
Without me, no one can go to the Father.*

*The Holy Bible: Contemporary English Version. Copyright © 1995, American Bible Society.
John 3:16; 14:6, quoted with permission.*

Not long after Jesus left them, his followers began to feel that his Holy Spirit had come back to them in a special way. They began to tell everyone that Jesus of Nazareth was the Christ, the great King and Anointed One whom God had promised to send.

More than that, Jesus' followers believed that in some unexplainable way Jesus was the very Son of God himself. His death on the cross had actually been a sacrifice, like the animal sacrifices offered in olden times. He had died to make *atonement*, so that sinful people could once again be *at-one* with God.

The news spread quickly, for it was good news. If you believed in Jesus Christ with all your heart, then you would be forgiven for all the wrong things you ever did or said or thought. You would know that Christ is with you in this world, to guide you and help you by his Holy Spirit. And when at last you leave this world by death, you would still have the sure hope of going to be with Christ in a better world, or *heaven*.

GOOD NEWS!

The good news about Jesus soon spread from Palestine into other parts of Asia, into North Africa, and into the whole continent of Europe.

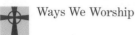
It took deepest roots in Europe, so that to this day many people think of Christianity as a religion only for white-skinned people. But from its very beginning, the way of the Christ has opened out into all the world.

The spread of Christianity.

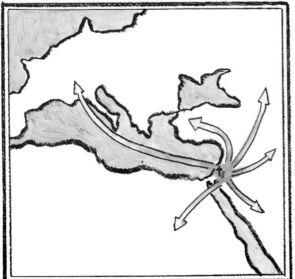

Some of the men and women who first helped spread the good news about Jesus the Christ had names that are still common on every continent today: Mark, Luke, Paul, Lydia, Priscilla, and Stephen. Besides telling about Jesus the Christ in spoken words, some of these people also wrote about him.

Luke, a Greek doctor, wrote one of the most detailed biographies of Jesus. He also wrote a history of the first half-century after Jesus lived on earth; it's called Acts of the Apostles, or Acts for short. (*Apostles* means sent-out ones, a name Jesus gave to his *disciples*, or followers, when he sent them out to tell the Good News.)

One Word, Two Meanings

Gospel: An old-fashioned English word translating a Greek word that means good news.

Gospel: The name of each of the four books in the New Testament that tell the Good News about Jesus Christ: The Gospel of (or written by) Matthew, the Gospel of Mark, the Gospel of Luke, and the Gospel of John.

The apostle Paul, another highly educated believer, wrote letters to church members in many places. He taught Christians many important truths about the way of the Christ.

The Most Famous Words Paul Ever Wrote

What if I could speak all languages of humans and of angels?
If I did not love others, I would be nothing more
than a noisy gong or a clanging cymbal.
What if I could prophesy
and understand all secrets and all knowledge?
And what if I had faith that moved mountains?
I would be nothing, unless I loved others.
Love is kind and patient, never jealous, boastful, proud, or rude.
Love isn't selfish or quick tempered.
It doesn't keep a record of wrongs that others do.
Love rejoices in the truth, but not in evil.
Love is always supportive, loyal, hopeful, and trusting.
Love never fails!

During the two thousand years since Jesus lived on this earth, Christian history has taken an amazing number of twists and turns. Those who follow the way of the Christ all read the same Scriptures and all honor the same founder of their religion; yet they are divided into hundreds of different ways of worshiping.

Let's try to get a clearer understanding of these many forms of Christianity by viewing them from three different directions:

- First, let's take a quick look at a few basics that all Christians believe and at what they do because of these beliefs.

- Next, let's look at three major groupings of similar churches and *denominations*, or types of churches.

- After that, let's look at several terms used nowadays to describe churches and individual Christians, no matter which of the three major groupings they may fit into.

WHAT ALL CHRISTIANS AGREE ABOUT

All Christians agree that Jesus the Christ is a special person. When the World Council of Churches got started in 1948, the one requirement for joining was to declare that Jesus Christ is "God and Savior."

Differences start to appear among Christians when they try to explain how it is that Jesus the Christ was God in the person of a human being and how it is that Jesus the Christ is the Savior today of those who believe in him.

All Christians agree that the Bible is a special book. No Christian would ever say, "The Bible doesn't matter any more; it's just a collection of ancient legends; it has nothing to say to people of this generation."

Differences start to appear among Christians when they try to explain how the Holy Bible came to be written, who wrote it, why it's so special, and how it should be read, explained, and applied to human life today.

All Christians agree that Jesus the Christ taught them to tell everybody everywhere the good news about him. When Christians tell non-Christians about their beliefs, it's not because they have no respect for other people's religions. It's because they're doing what Jesus commanded them to do. By obeying this command, Christians have spread their way of worshiping into every continent on the globe.

Differences start to appear among Christians when they try to explain exactly what is included in the good news about Jesus and exactly how they should share this good news with other people.

Almost all Christians agree that they should perform two special ceremonies as taught by Jesus the Christ. These ceremonies are *baptism*, which happens only once in a Christian's life, and *the Lord's Supper*, which is repeated many times.

■ Baptism involves putting a person into water, or pouring or sprinkling water on a person; it is a way of saying, "This person now belongs to the Christ." Some Christians baptize babies (in a ceremony sometimes called a *christening*); later on, a boy or girl who was baptized as a baby may have a special *confirmation* service, to make his or her faith *firm*. Other Christians baptize only people already old enough to say for themselves, "I am a follower of the Christ."

■ The Lord's Supper is a special meal eaten together by Christians. It is also called *Holy Communion* or the *Holy Eucharist*. Broken bread reminds Christians of Jesus' body broken on the cross. Red wine or grape juice reminds them of Jesus' blood.

Differences start to appear among Christians when they try to explain how old a person should be when baptized, how baptism should be done, what baptism really means, what the Lord's Supper really means, and who should take the Lord's Supper together. (A few groups of Christians, such as the Friends or Quakers, do not perform these ceremonies.)

THE CATHOLIC WAY

The word *catholic* means universal or general. Nobody needed to use such a word at first because there were no divisions among the first followers of the Christ. Christianity was called simply "the Faith" or "the Way" (see Acts of the Apostles in the Holy Bible, chapter 6, verse 7, and chapter 9, verse 2).

Acts chapter 11 tells us when and where followers of Jesus were first called *Christians* (little Christs or members of Christ's party). It was in the great city of Antioch, near the Mediterranean coast of Syria.

It didn't take long for Christians to start splitting up into different groups. Sometimes this happened because different church leaders thought that different parts of Jesus' teachings were the most important parts. Sometimes it happened just because different churches developed at different times and places, where people lived in different ways.

Most Christians wanted to keep up their connections with other believers who lived in other places. They began to choose managers (sometimes called *bishops*) to help things run more smoothly. To make

The Pope is the leader of the Roman Catholic Church.

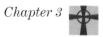

sure no one thought they were part of a breakaway group, they began to call themselves *Catholic* Christians: universal or general Christians.

Gradually the great capital city of the Roman Empire became the most important center for Christianity. And gradually the bishop of Rome became the most important of all the bishops. Christians began to call him *Papa*, or Father; in English we say Pope.

Through the long centuries, Catholics have developed in ways that have influenced the whole world. Columbus and many other explorers set sail, not just to seek their fortunes but to find new lands to conquer for Christ. The shape of many present-day church buildings, inside and out, still looks more or less like the churches Catholics were already building hundreds of years ago. Some of the world's most beautiful music was first written to be played and sung in Catholic churches. Some of the world's finest paintings and statues were made by Catholic artists.

Today the Roman Catholic Church is the largest of all denominations, or groups of churches. All Roman Catholics honor the Pope, the bishop of Rome, as their earthly head. Great Popes of the twentieth century have led Catholic church members to spend more time reading the Holy Bible, and making its teachings an important part of their lives.

(Now, here's something most people don't know: Besides the huge Roman Catholic Church, there are also several smaller Catholic denominations that don't necessarily recognize the Pope as their spiritual leader. Among these are the Independent Catholics of the Philippines, the Anglo-Catholics of England and the United States, and some of the Catholics of China.)

THE ORTHODOX WAY

The word *orthodox* means praising (or worshiping) in the right way. During the first centuries of Christian history, the great Roman Empire split into two halves, west and east. The Roman Catholic Church grew up in the western half, where Rome was still the main center. But there were also many Christians in the eastern half. These eastern Christians were separated from the Roman Catholics—first by distance and later by time. Slowly they developed a different way of looking at things.

As you remember the meaning of orthodox, you should be able to guess that Orthodox Christians make worship services an unusually important part of their lives. They also make an especially big thing of Christ's resurrection, or rising again from death. (By contrast, Roman Catholics make an especially big thing of Christ's crucifixion, or dying on the cross.) Orthodox Christians do not recognize a single Pope. Instead, they honor several top-level church leaders called *patriarchs* (fathers).

By the time a thousand years had passed, Christians of the West (Roman Catholics) and Christians of the East had become completely separated. Two important countries in the eastern half of Europe are Greece and Russia. That's why this major grouping of Christians is sometimes called Eastern Orthodox, Greek Orthodox, or Russian Orthodox. As a matter of fact there are also many other Orthodox churches, such as the Bulgarian Orthodox, the Serbian Orthodox, the Ethiopian Orthodox, the Armenian Apostolic Church, and the Coptic Christians of Egypt.

One of the most amazing chapters in the long history of Orthodox Christianity was written in the twentieth century. For seventy years the Soviet Union tried to wipe out the way of the Christ. About 200,000 church leaders were killed—shot, scalped, strangled, crucified, frozen into columns of ice. Millions of ordinary Christians also died for their faith; forty thousand church buildings were destroyed. Yet, when communism fell in 1989, the Russian Orthodox Church was still alive and well.

THE PROTESTANT WAY

The term *Protestant* first began to be used about five hundred years ago, when many Christians in Europe began protesting against the Roman Catholic Church. They felt that Catholics had moved too far away from the simple teachings of Jesus. They accused many church leaders of being no better than earthly kings.

This new movement in the 1500s was called the *Protestant Reformation*. Two of its greatest leaders were *Martin Luther* in Germany and *John*

Three Groups with Out-of-Date Names

The old names still being used for the three main groups of Christians don't really mean that much any more:

- **Catholic** no longer means universal or general, because not all followers of the Christ are Catholics.
- **Orthodox** no longer means that only members of Orthodox churches are praising or worshiping God in the "right" way.
- **Protestant** no longer means protesting, because most Protestant Christians aren't still opposed to Catholic Christians today.

Calvin in France and Switzerland. Both of them taught that people get into a right relationship with God by believing and trusting in him, not by keeping church rules. They also taught that every person can relate directly to God through Jesus Christ, without needing a human go-between. (This is one of the reasons why the leader of a local group of Protestant Christians is usually called a *pastor*, meaning a shepherd, rather than being called a *priest* as in most Catholic and Orthodox churches.)

Probably most of the non-Catholic churches you may happen to know about are Protestant churches. Some of them might not like to be called Protestant; notice several other terms explained in the next section of this chapter. This book uses the term Protestant to include all those who follow Jesus Christ as Lord and God and Savior but who do not worship in the Catholic way or the Orthodox way.

How many different kinds of Protestants are there? That's a hard one to answer. Besides all the churches and denominations that are well known in the United States, there are many other Protestant groups most Americans know nothing about. For instance: Have you ever heard of the Word of Life Church in Ethiopia? or the Batak Church in Sumatra, Indonesia? or the Kimbanguist Church in Zaire, Central Africa? Each of these Protestant denominations has millions of members.

Here's a list of some (not nearly all!) of the names used by Protestant churches and denominations in the United States:

Adventist	Christian	Evangelical	Moravian
Amish	Christian and Missionary Alliance	Foursquare Gospel	Nazarenes
Anglican		Friends (Quakers)	Pentecostal
Assemblies of God	Church of Christ	Holiness	Presbyterian
Baptist	Church of God	Lutheran	Reformed
Bible	Congregational	Mennonite	Salvation Army
Brethren	Disciples of Christ	Methodist	Wesleyan
	Episcopal		

OTHER WAYS OF GROUPING CHRISTIANS

In the twentieth century, Christians began to use new words to describe themselves—words that might not have anything to do with which churches they were members of. Let's take a look at some of these terms:

ECUMENICAL

Many followers of Jesus Christ feel sad and ashamed because there are so many different kinds of Christians. They like to plan ways different kinds of Christians can meet together and work together. Sometimes they even plan ways several denominations can be joined together into one. This twentieth-century trend in Christianity is called the *ecumenical movement.*

The best-known result of the ecumenical movement is the World Council of Churches, founded in 1948. Smaller councils or fellowships of churches also work together in many nations of the world. But the ecumenical movement has had other results as well.

Some Christians like to work together mainly with other Christians that use the same name. For instance, many different kinds of Lutherans cooperate through the Lutheran World Federation. Many different kinds of Baptists meet together in the Baptist World Alliance.

Some Christians like to work together mainly to carry out certain jobs, such as telling the good news about Jesus all over the world, sharing food with hungry people in Jesus' name, building houses for the homeless, or meeting other human needs.

Remember: The word *ecumenical* doesn't mean a new and different church or grouping of churches. You might meet an ecumenical Methodist or an ecumenical Presbyterian or an ecumenical Orthodox Christian.

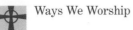

Ecumenical isn't the only present-day term that stretches across from one denomination to another.

CHARISMATIC

Do you remember what the title "Christ" really means? Can you see some of those same letters in the same order, in the first part of the word *charismatic*?

A charismatic Christian is one who thinks it's very important to be *anointed* by Christ's Holy Spirit. You might see and hear this special touch of the Spirit when a charismatic worships—with clapping, with hands and face raised toward heaven, sometimes even with falling to the floor half conscious because of strong religious emotions. Some charismatics heal sick people without medicine, speak in languages they have never learned, or know important things no one has ever told them.

The modern charismatic movement began early in the twentieth century. It caused the starting of several new denominations with names like Pentecostal, Church of God, and Assemblies of God.

Then in the middle of the twentieth century, charismatic ideas began to move into other kinds of churches. Today you might meet a charismatic Baptist, a charismatic Roman Catholic, or a charismatic member of the Episcopal Church.

Sometimes charismatic Christians stay in the churches where they are already members, but they also start small groups that meet in people's homes. There they can enjoy fellowship with other Christians who feel their faith in the same way.

Sometimes charismatic Christians feel that members of the old familiar churches have lost any real sense that the Christ is living within them through his Holy Spirit. So they pull out and start new denominations, such as the Vineyard Fellowship or People of Destiny International.

Sometimes they start independent churches, not joined with any denomination. The largest church in the world today is an independent charismatic church in Seoul, South Korea.

EVANGELICAL

Some Protestants don't like to be called Protestants. That old-fashioned name makes it sound like all they ever do is make a protest about something. Many prefer the term *evangelical*; it comes from the same Greek word for good news, which was also translated by the old English word gospel.

"*Protestant* sounds too negative," so these Christians might say. "We're evangelicals. For us, the most important thing is telling everybody everywhere the Good News about Jesus Christ."

Each evangelical Christian has made a personal decision to turn the control of his or her life over to Jesus the Christ. When this happens, they say, "It's like being *born again*."

As you might expect, it's mainly evangelical Christians who support *missionaries*, both in their own homeland and in foreign countries.

A missionary tells people about Jesus.

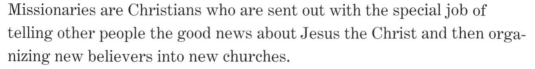

Missionaries are Christians who are sent out with the special job of telling other people the good news about Jesus the Christ and then organizing new believers into new churches.

Like the other terms you've been reading about, *evangelical* doesn't mean only one kind of Christian or only one type of church. Some entire denominations might be called charismatic; some entire denominations might also be called evangelical—for instance, the Christian and Missionary Alliance or the Salvation Army. But there are evangelical Christians in almost all types of churches.

FUNDAMENTALIST, CONSERVATIVE, MODERATE, LIBERAL

Don't make a big mistake here: These four terms do NOT mean the same thing. Instead, think of this list of four names as a sort of graph, moving across the page from one side to the other.

Fundamentalist Christians hold strongly to beliefs they think to be most *fundamental*—the very foundations of their faith. They believe every word of the Holy Bible, just as it is written. They're ready to stand up and fight against people who don't pay much attention to the Bible. Often fundamentalists will argue that a pregnant woman has no right to an abortion because that's the same as murdering her baby. Fundamentalists will also often argue against alternative life-styles, because they believe the Bible says such ways of living are wrong.

Conservative Christians may believe many of the same things fundamentalists do, but they're not as likely to argue about their beliefs. Conservatives try to *conserve* the traditional message of the Bible, as well as *conserve* traditional ways of acting out that message in everyday life.

The word *liberal* means free. As you might expect, liberals are a lot more *free* than other Christians in how they read the Bible, or how they

Symbols of the Christ

Through the years Christians have used many symbols. Some of these come from Greek, the language spoken by many of Jesus' first followers. You will often see these symbols—in churches as well as in other places.

These three letters look like the first three letters of the name **Jesus** in Greek.

These letters that look like **X** and **P** are actually the first two letters of **Christ** in Greek.

The familiar sign of the fish was first used by Christians as a sort of secret code. The Greek word for fish, **ichthus**, actually has only five letters in Greek. The same five letters are also the first letters of five important words: **I**esous (Jesus) **CH**ristos (Christ), **TH**eou (God's) **U**ios (Son), **S**oter (Savior).

put its message to work. Liberals don't necessarily believe every word that's written in the Bible. And they certainly don't agree with many old-fashioned Christian ideas.

How about *moderate*, the one term we skipped over in that list of four names? You can probably guess: A moderate is a Christian who takes a middle position on the graph between fundamentalists and conservatives on one side and liberals on the other. A moderate Christian tries to *moderate*, or adjust or adapt, things from both sides that are good and important.

This list or graph of terms has become highly important to many Christians in recent years. When they look for a church to join, they don't ask what denomination the church belongs to, such as Baptist, Methodist, or Presbyterian. Instead, they want to know whether the church is fundamentalist, conservative, moderate, or liberal.

You can find churches of all four kinds in many different denominations —both Protestant and Catholic. Even within the same church, you can find individual Christians who are fundamentalists, conservatives, moderates, or liberals.

THE WAY OF THE CHRIST TODAY

Do you realize what a big influence the way of the Christ has had on the world of today? Through the centuries Christians haven't just started churches: They've also started many of the world's schools, universities, hospitals, and shelters for homeless children. They've climbed the highest mountains and crossed the widest oceans to tell the good news about Jesus the Christ.

A short list of famous twentieth-century Christians would include familiar names:

- *Mother Teresa of Calcutta*, the tiny Roman Catholic *nun* (or unmarried woman giving her whole life to her way of worshiping) who left her home and family in Europe to go and help the sick and dying on the streets of one of Asia's neediest cities.

- *Martin Luther King, Jr.*, the Baptist preacher who lived and died so that his fellow Americans would judge people by the content of their character rather than by the color of their skin.

- Evangelists such as *Billy Graham* of the United States and *Luis Palau* of Argentina, who have led great multimedia campaigns on many continents, telling millions of people why Jesus the Christ came into our world.

- Karol Wojtyla, the friendly priest from Poland who became *Pope John Paul II*, traveling the globe with a message of goodness and good will.

- *Desmond Tutu*, the bishop who has led the fight to turn South Africans away from dividing people according to their race.

- Former American president *Jimmy Carter*, who has helped people make peace and hold honest elections all over the globe.

Not everything is rosy for those who follow the way of the Christ in our world today:

- Catholics and Protestants have found it hard to live together as peaceful neighbors in such places as Ireland.

- Christians and Muslims have made trouble for one another in Bosnia, Sudan, Nigeria, Indonesia, and dozens of other countries.

- Many people who call themselves Christians seem to know little of what Jesus taught and even less of the love Jesus showed.

■ Many Christians live in lands where they dare not let anyone else know about their way of worshiping.

Yet, it seems only fair to say that Christians have more influence in the modern world than followers of any other religion. One reason is that there are more Christians than there are people who worship in any other way—many more!

The two largest religions in the world are Islam and Christianity. But there are nearly twice as many Christians as there are Muslims in the world today. One third of all the people on earth claim to follow the way of the Christ—nearly two billion men and women, boys and girls.

An important change has come over world Christianity during the past hundred years or so. In the 1890s, most Christians lived in Europe or in places where Europeans had settled—the Americas, Australia, New Zealand. By the 1990s, two thirds of all Christians lived in other parts of the world—especially in Africa and Asia.

Most people don't think of Mainland China when they think of Christianity. Yet the fact is, by the 1990s there may have been as many as seventy-five million Christians living in that huge Asian nation.

Wherever you go in the world today, you're likely to meet Christians. They come in all sizes, all colors, all traditions. The only thing that makes them one is what the apostle Paul wrote two thousand years ago:

"If you honestly say, 'Jesus is Lord,' and if you believe with all your heart that God raised him from death,"* then you will be saved—in this world, and also in the world yet to come.

*Romans 10:9 in The Holy Bible: Contemporary English Version; copyright © 1995, American Bible Society; quoted with permission.

Milestones Along the Way of the Christ

Being born: Many Christians—Catholic, Orthodox, and Protestant—baptize babies. (On page 51 you can read about baptism and christening.) Other Christians, including many Protestants and evangelicals, may instead bring babies to church to dedicate them to God in a special time of worship.

Joining the worshiping community: (On page 51 you can read about baptism and confirmation.)

Getting married: Many Christians of all types get married at a church, with a pastor, priest, or other minister in charge. Brides usually wear white. The church is often decorated with flowers, greenery, and lighted candles. Family and friends enjoy a party or reception afterward.

Dying: Christians sometimes wait to bury a dead body till all the members of the family can gather together. A pastor, priest, or other minister usually leads a funeral service—sometimes at a church, sometimes at a special funeral home. Afterward, everyone rides in a long procession of cars to the cemetery, where another short service of worship and memory is usually held beside the open grave.

4 The Way of Islam

"That's the Moslems' church," said Lane, pointing toward a brick building set back from the street.

"Huh! Moslems must not be very good builders," Joey remarked. "Look, they put it sideways on the lot!"

"Well," Lane replied, "what can you expect of people who pray to Mohammed?"

"I thought their god was named Allah," Joey argued. "But anyhow, aren't they those guys that are always starting wars? Like in the Persian Gulf, and in Bosnia?"

Lane shrugged. "Moslems are different, that's all; they're just not our kind of people."

If you are a *Muslim* (a better spelling and pronunciation than *Moslem*), or if you even have a friend or neighbor who is a Muslim, what you have just read probably made you mad, or sad, or both. That imaginary conversation was put at the beginning of this chapter as a warning: Probably more people have more wrong ideas about Muslims than about followers of any other religion.

Let's see if we can correct some of the wrong ideas that turned up when Lane and Joey were having that little talk.

■ A Muslim place of worship is not a church; it's called a *masjid* or a mosque. Both words mean the place where people bow down in prayer, which is one of the things Muslims do as a part of their worship.

■ Muslims are great builders; they built the Taj Mahal, which many people think is the most beautiful building in the world (see the picture on p. 67). But there's a special reason why a masjid sometimes seems to sit "sideways on the lot": It's always built at the proper angle so that worshipers inside it can face toward a certain direction as they pray.

■ Muslims do not pray to *Muhammad* (a better spelling and pronunciation than *Mohammed*); they love and honor him as the human being who was chosen to bring their religion to the world.

■ *Allah* is not "the Muslims' god"; that name comes from Arabic words meaning *the* God, the only God there is. Millions of Christians, in Indonesia and other countries, also use Allah as their name for the one Lord God.

■ How about Muslims starting wars? Look closely at the correct name for the Muslim way of worshiping: *Islam*. Do you see the letters *s-l-m*, in the same order as in the Hebrew word *shalom*, peace? Both words come from the same root. And most of those who worship in the way of Islam like to live in peace just as much as other people do. (By the way, Muslims didn't start the war in Bosnia; they have mostly been the victims of that war. In the Persian Gulf War, there were Muslims and Christians fighting on both sides.)

◼ How about that last remark in our imaginary conversation? Are Muslims really all that "different"? Are they "not our kind of people"?

Sometimes light-skinned Americans may get ideas like that because most of the Muslims they happen to know are either dark-skinned Americans or else newcomers to America. But the fact is, Islam—like Christianity—has spread all over the world. Muslims—like Christians—come in all colors.

What is this way of worshipping that so many people seem to misunderstand? When and where did it get started?

Like the way of Judaism and the way of the Christ, the way of Islam also got started in the Middle East . . . but farther south, nearer the equator.

IN "THE ISLAND OF ARABIA"

If you look at the Arabian peninsula on a map, you can see why Arabs themselves call it "the Island of Arabia." Arabia is cut off from the rest of the world—by sea on three sides and by sand on the fourth side. No rivers flow through the Arabian desert.

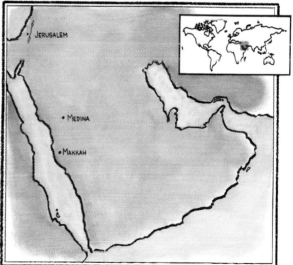

There are few places where people can settle down and grow crops. No wonder many Arabs through the centuries have lived as wandering nomads.

Trying to survive in such a place, most Arabs in olden times looked out only for themselves. Often one clan leader would pick a fight with another. Arguments heated up into tribal wars. No family was safe from raiders; they might lose their camels, their goats, even their women and children.

Religion? Oh, the ancient Arabs were religious, all right: They had gods for the stars, for the moon, for almost everything they saw in nature. Above all of these was a greater god, but the Arabs knew almost nothing about that one—certainly not enough to make an idol to be worshiped.

Here and there, wells and underground streams make a green oasis in the dry heat of Arabia. One such oasis is the ancient city of Makkah or Mecca, near the Red Sea. In 570 A.D., people of Makkah knew a bit more about the world outside "the Island of Arabia" than most other desert folk did: Makkah was a major stop for spice caravans. Also, Makkah was a center for worship. Religious pilgrims came there from all over Arabia.

In the main square of Makkah stood a temple called the *Kaaba* or Cube, for it was shaped like a big black block. No one knew for sure who had built it, when or why. Everyone agreed that it was holy, but so was all of Makkah. In that city stood 360 places for worshiping 360 different idol-gods—one for each day of the lunar year. (The ancient Arabs, like their cousins the ancient Hebrews, followed a calendar based on when the new moon appeared in the sky.)

It was in the holy city of Makkah that an Arab boy was born in 570 A.D. Later in life he was given the name *Muhammad*: "one who is highly praised." (In the fourteen centuries since then, more boys have been given that name than any other name in the whole world.)

Muhammad came from a poor but honest family. His childhood wasn't easy: His father died before he was born. His mother died when he was six; his grandfather, when he was eight. After that, he lived with his uncle. He had to go to work early—first as a goatherd and then as a camel driver. No one ever bothered to teach him how to read and write.

As a young man, Muhammad began working for a rich widow. She noticed his hard work, his honesty, his courage. Before long, they got married. Several children were born, but most of them died young.

When Muhammad was almost forty years old, he began to have strange visions. An angel came to him, telling him the true way of worshiping. At first Muhammad was frightened. He thought he might be going crazy. He wondered why he of all people had been picked for such an unusual experience. But his wife encouraged him. Gradually he came to understand that he had been chosen to deliver a special message.

The most important thing he learned was this: *God is One.* Muhammad had met people who followed the way of Judaism and people who followed the way of the Christ. He had heard about the one Lord God worshiped by the Jews. Now he realized that *Allah*—the far-distant One for whom no Arab ever made an idol—was indeed "*the* God," the only God there is.

The angel who appeared to Muhammad told him about a holy book in heaven. He taught Muhammad to repeat or recite after him words from this book. That's why the Muslims' sacred book is called the *Glorious Qur'an* (a better spelling than *Koran*), from the Arabic word meaning to recite. Muhammad memorized what he heard the angel say. Then he passed it on to others, who eventually began to write it down—on stones, on camel bones, on sheets of leather.

"No more idols!" Muhammad began preaching to the people of Makkah. "No more lying or gambling or stealing or killing! There is no God but Allah, and Allah demands that you live clean lives!"

Who Is Allah?

Allah is the Holy, the Peaceful, the Faithful,
the One who guards his servants,
the One who shelters orphans,
the One who guides those who miss the right way;
the One who rescues from every difficulty,
the One who is a friend to those in sorrow,
the One who comforts those in trouble.
Allah gives good things; he is the generous Lord,
the gracious One, the One who hears,
the One near-at-hand, the compassionate One,
the merciful One, the very-forgiving One.
Allah's love for humanity is more tender
than the love of a mother bird for her young.

Reworded and abridged from the Glorious Qur'an.

Not many people believed him at first. In three years he gained only forty followers. Other people in Makkah made fun of him. They began to throw dirt when he and his friends would gather for worship. So in the year 622 A.D. Muhammad led his little group to another city, several days' camel ride to the north. There he found people who would listen to his teaching.

Muslims of today count years in two different ways. For ordinary purposes they use A.D. just as others do. But for dating their religious festivals, they use *A.H.*, counting from the time when Muhammad and his followers made their escape from Makkah. (The *H.* stands for *hijra* or *hegira*, an Arabic word meaning flight or escape.)

The city in northern Arabia that became Muhammad's new home used to have another name, but it soon came to be called the City of the Prophet, or *Medina*, "the City," for short. What a change came over Medina during those few years when Muhammad was its leader! Arabs began to treat each other as brothers instead of as enemies. They did away with idols and began to worship the one Lord God.

The people of Makkah got worried. They thought Muhammad was planning to stir up a clan war against them. So they tried to conquer Medina, but ended up being conquered themselves. By the year 630 A.D. Muhammad took charge of both cities. He pulled the idols out of the Kaaba and smashed them in the public square of Makkah. He explained that the ancient black cube was really a place for worshiping Allah alone.

Muhammad also explained parts of the Jewish Scriptures in a different way from Jews or Christians. The book of Genesis tells us that Abraham, the founding father of the Jewish people, had a son named Ishmael. But Ishmael's mother was a slave-girl named Hagar, so Abraham still waited for another son from his legal wife, Sarah. Finally that son was born and was named Isaac. Because of Sarah's jealousy, Hagar and Ishmael were then driven away from Abraham's tent.

Muhammad taught that when Hagar and Ishmael wandered through the desert, they found water at an oasis: the well around which the city of Makkah later grew up. He also taught that it was really Ishmael, not Isaac, who was nearly killed by his father as a sacrifice. So Jerusalem, where Abraham's altar of sacrifice had stood, became just as special for Muslims as for Jews.

It wasn't only stories from the Jewish Scriptures that Muhammad explained in a new and different way. He taught his followers to honor such famous Bible characters as Moses, Aaron, and David; he also

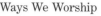

taught them to honor Jesus the Christ. "But," said Muhammad, "Jesus was only a great prophet; he was not the Savior. And certainly he was not God: There is no God but Allah!"

Jews and Christians followed holy writings, so Muhammad began to call them People of the Book. Most of the time he treated Jews and Christians kindly. But he also warned them that they should follow the Islamic way of worshiping, along with his fellow Arabs who had been worshiping idols.

People of the Book

What sacred writings do Jews, Christians, and Muslims use in their religions?

	Jews	Christians	Muslims
The Holy Bible:			
Old Testament	Yes	Yes	Yes, but in a different way from Jews and Christians
New Testament	No	Yes	Yes, but in a different way from Christians
The Glorious Qur'an	No	No	Yes

Muhammad died suddenly in 632 A.D. His followers kept on in the way of living and worshiping he had taught them. They carefully put his teachings together in clear written form.

The religion Muhammad had taught them was called *Islam*. This Arabic word means submission, but it also (like the similar Hebrew word *shalom*) means peace.

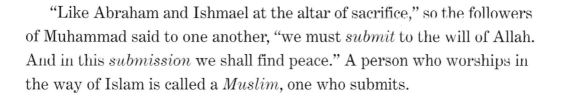

"Like Abraham and Ishmael at the altar of sacrifice," so the followers of Muhammad said to one another, "we must *submit* to the will of Allah. And in this *submission* we shall find peace." A person who worships in the way of Islam is called a *Muslim*, one who submits.

MUSLIMS ON THE MOVE

Islam isn't just a religion; it's a whole way of life. A Muslim may wonder why other people seem to pay so little attention to their way of worshiping except on one day a week. A Muslim may also find it hard to understand how religion can be separated from law and order, from peace and justice. For a Muslim, it's all one and the same. The Glorious Qur'an and other Islamic teachings explain what everybody is supposed to do—everywhere, every day.

With this way of looking at the world, it isn't surprising that Islam quickly spread from "the Island of Arabia." If Allah is the only true God, and if Allah will sit in judgment over everyone, then people everywhere must be warned—whether they want to hear about it or not.

Many of the Arabs' neighbors were willing enough to become Muslim converts. Better to worship one God than many; better to treat other people as brothers than as enemies. Also, kings of neighboring lands—some of them Christians—had made life hard for ordinary folks. Often these people felt that the Arab armies had come to set them free. Sometimes, it is true, the coming of the conquering Arab armies caused people to become Muslims; in those days the same sort of thing often happened when Christian armies were on the winning side.

Riding their swift desert horses, the Arabs swept across all of the Middle East and North Africa. Within less than a hundred years after the

death of Muhammad, they had worked their way westward to the Straits of Gibraltar, and even across the Straits into Spain. Only a horrendous battle in 732 A.D. kept them from conquering France as well. Even so, Muslims already controlled more territory than the Roman Empire ever did.

Islam also moved out to the east and the north and the south, as well as to the west. People living in the countries now known as Iraq, Iran, Afghanistan, and Pakistan soon became Muslims, and they are still mostly Muslims today. Millions of Muslims also live in India, Bangladesh, Malaysia, the Philippines, China, and other countries of Asia. On the islands of Indonesia, scattered from the Indian Ocean to the South Pacific, there are more Muslims today than in any other country on earth.

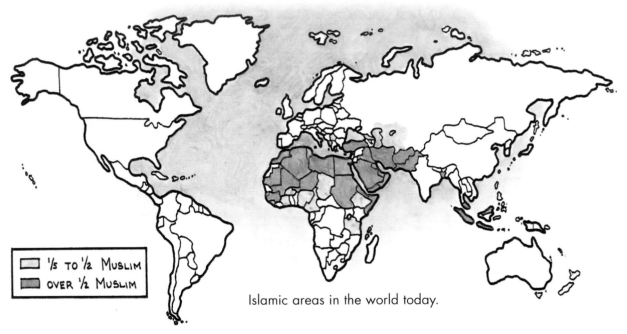

Islamic areas in the world today.

ISLAM: A WAY OF LIFE

What is this way of worshiping, this way of life that reached so many people in such a short period of history? How do you get to be a Muslim, anyway?

It's really quite simple. In the presence of at least two other Muslims, you must say (and really believe it): "There is no God but Allah, and Muhammad is Allah's messenger." (The Arabic word for *messenger* is sometimes translated as "prophet." Muslims believe that Muhammad was the last—and greatest—of a long line of Allah's prophets.)

After that, you must try to live the rest of your life according to the *Five Pillars* (or five foundation stones) of Islam:

1. You've already done the first one, in stating publicly the heart of what you believe.

2. Five times a day, you should pray. If you live near a masjid, you may hear the call to prayer from its *minaret* or steeple—at sunset, at bedtime, before daybreak, at noon, and in mid-afternoon. Before praying, you should wash your head, arms, and feet. Then you should recite parts of the Glorious Qur'an and pray while following the correct order of standing, bending, sitting, and bowing down toward the Kaaba in the holy city of Makkah. Prayers every Friday noon are best if done with other Muslims at the masjid. An *imam*, a man who makes a special study of your religion, may lead the prayers and preach a sermon based on verses from the Qur'an.

Muslim men bowing down in prayer.

3. During one month of the year according to the Muslim calendar, you should go without eating or drinking during daylight hours. This will help you remember the time when Allah first sent an angel to give Muhammad the words recited from the original Qur'an in heaven.

4. You ought to remember that Allah has given you everything you have. Because of this, you should be willing to share with others. As a Muslim you should give offerings of food and money—to help sick people, poor people, widows, and orphans.

5. Once in your lifetime—if you have the strength and the money to do it—you should go as a pilgrim to the holy city of Makkah. There you will see the sacred well where Hagar and Ishmael found water in the desert. There you will walk seven times around the Kaaba, the great black cube. There you will sacrifice a goat or sheep or other animal, as Abraham did so long ago.

The Biggest Day of the Year for Muslims

Like Christians and Jews, Muslims have several special days. By far the biggest day of the year for Muslims is **Idul Fitri**, which comes at the end of the month of doing without food during daylight hours.

For Muslims, **Idul Fitri** is a lot like Christmas and New Year's; they celebrate with feasts, visits, parties, and gifts. The date for **Idul Fitri** is set by the Muslim lunar calendar; each year it comes about eleven days earlier than the year before.

An important part of **Idul Fitri** is asking other people to forgive you for anything wrong you may have done to them during the past year—and, of course, forgiving them also if they have done anything wrong to you.

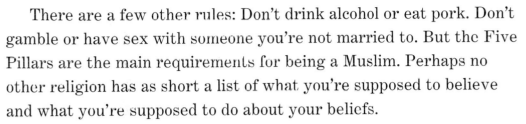

There are a few other rules: Don't drink alcohol or eat pork. Don't gamble or have sex with someone you're not married to. But the Five Pillars are the main requirements for being a Muslim. Perhaps no other religion has as short a list of what you're supposed to believe and what you're supposed to do about your beliefs.

This is one reason why many people become Muslims. They like the way of Islam because it seems simple and clear.

Another thing is also clear to Muslims: There will come a day when Allah will judge every human being according to what he or she has done in this world. Only those who have followed the way of Islam, who have submitted themselves to Allah, will be welcomed into *paradise*, or heaven. Christ also taught of a coming day of judgment, but many Christians seem not to remember this as much as Muslims do. No wonder Muslims want other people to become Muslims, too!

The Day of Doom

Praise belongs to God, the Lord of all being,
the all-merciful One, the all-compassionate One,
the Master of the Day of Doom.
When the sun shall be darkened,
when the stars shall be thrown down,
when the mountains shall be set moving,
when the seas shall be set boiling,
when hell shall be set blazing,
when paradise shall be brought near,
Then you will know what you have produced!

Reworded and abridged from the Glorious Qur'an.

ISLAMIC CIVILIZATIONS

A thousand years passed after the lifetimes of Muhammad and his first followers. During much of that time, Muslim countries became richer then most of the countries of Europe. They developed more advanced civilizations, too. They built great cities with street lights, running water, public baths, libraries with classified books, and palaces of fabulous beauty.

Muslim doctors, astronomers, and mapmakers became world-famous. They translated much of the wisdom of the Greeks and Romans into Arabic; if they hadn't, that ancient learning would have been lost forever. They also added their own wisdom, based on the teachings of Islam.

Even some of the words we use today came from wise Muslims of long ago who wrote in Arabic: *almanac, algebra, zero, zenith*. And not just the words themselves: Muslim scientists understood the ideas behind those words.

Muslims taught Europeans how to build with pointed arches, how to send messages in battle via carrier pigeon, and how to sweeten foods with oranges and apricots and sugar. The very numbers we use today were first developed by Muslim math experts; that's why we call them Arabic numerals.

Yet, relations between Muslims and their non-Muslim neighbors didn't always run smoothly during the Middle Ages. Christians of Europe decided that only they should control Palestine, the land where Christ lived on earth. This led to a long series of wars called the *Crusades*. Muslims tried to take over all of eastern Europe and managed to conquer a few parts of it that are still Muslim to this day.

About a thousand years after the time when Muhammad lived, Islam seemed to be slowly fading away. Muslims had been driven out of Spain and most other parts of Europe. Muslim lands in Africa and Asia had mostly been conquered by European empires and made into colonies.

Nowadays all of that has changed. Three big developments in recent history have caused Islam to take on new importance all over the world:

1. Groups of Muslims began to go back to their roots. They began to call for people to follow the simple, clear teachings of Muhammad and his first desert disciples, without all the later additions. Like Christians who place great importance on the basic foundations of their faith, such Muslims are called *fundamentalists* or *conservatives*.
2. Like other former colonies all over the world, Muslim countries began to gain their freedom from European empires.
3. The modern world began to discover how much it needed petroleum to keep its machines running. Some of the lands where Muslims were strongest turned out to be the places that also had a lot of oil.

Today Islam is on the move all over the globe. Oil money from the Middle East helps pay for new masjids and new Islamic schools and centers—from Indonesia to England, from Nigeria to Canada. Thirteen million Muslims live in Europe, and five and a half million live in North America. Islam has become the second largest way of worshiping in the world. Only the way of the Christ has more followers.

MISTAKEN IDEAS ABOUT MUSLIMS

Remember that imaginary conversation at the very beginning of this chapter? Remember some of those mistaken ideas Lane and Joey had about Muslims?

Young people aren't the only ones who get wrong ideas about Muslims. Older people also misunderstand many things about those who follow the way of Islam. Here are a few of the questions people often ask:

❏ *Question #1:* Aren't all Muslims all over the world exactly the same? They're not split up into different groups like Christians and Jews, are they?

◆ *Fact:* Muslims began to separate soon after the death of Muhammad. Today they are divided into two major types, plus many smaller groups.

One of Muhammad's first followers was his eleven-year-old cousin, Ali. Later Ali married Muhammad's daughter, Fatima, and they had two sons. Many Muslims thought that these members of the great Prophet's own family should become their leaders. But Ali was murdered, and his sons also died—one of them in a bloody battle.

Millions of Muslims still remember that massacre of Muhammad's grandson and his followers. They call themselves *Shi'ites* (or *Shi'a* or *Shi'ah*), meaning partisans, or those who take the part of Ali and his sons.

Shi'ites perform the same Five Pillars of Islam that other Muslims do, but they let their religious leaders have great power over their lives. The Ayatollah Khomeini, who used to be the spiritual ruler of Iran, was a

Muslim of the Shi'ite type. Most Iranians today are Shi'ite Muslims; so are more than half of all Iraqis.

But there are many more Muslims of the *Sunnite* (or *Sunni*) type than of the Shi'ite type. The name *Sunnite* comes from a word that means tradition. The Sunnites feel that they are the ones following the true traditions handed down from Muhammad and his friends.

Besides these two main types, there are also many smaller groups of Muslims such as the Ismailis, the Ibadis, the Wahhabis, the Alawites, and the Druze. As you have already read, there are Muslim fundamentalists who say, "Let's go back to the basics of our faith." And there are still other Muslims who say, "What's really important is what you feel deep inside yourself, not the outward things you do."

For hundreds of years there have been Muslims who have said that inner feelings or spiritual things are what is important in religion. In the old desert days, these Muslims liked to wear simple woolen clothing, not richly embroidered robes. That's how they got the name *Sufi*, from the Arabic word for wool. One of the greatest of the Sufi poets was an eighth-century woman named Rabi'a.

❏ ***Question #2:*** Isn't it true that Muslim women and girls are treated like second-class citizens?

◆ ***Fact:*** Women and girls hold an important place in the way of Islam.

Remember the situation in Arabia before Muhammad began teaching and preaching? In those days women and girls were looked down on as mere property; they could be stolen or abused, and nobody seemed to care. Unwanted baby girls were sometimes even buried alive.

Muhammad changed all of that. He taught that women and girls should be respected. He taught that sisters should inherit from parents along with their brothers. He taught that no one should have a sexual partner outside of lawful marriage.

Two Prayers of Rabi'a

O my Lord, if I worship you from fear of hell,
then burn me in hell;
and if I worship you from hope of paradise,
then shut me out of paradise;
but if I worship you for your own sake,
then do not shut me out from your eternal beauty!

My God and my Lord: eyes are at rest, the stars are setting,
hushed are the movements of birds in their nests.
And you are the just One that knows no change,
the everlasting One that never passes away.
The doors of kings are locked and guarded,
but your door is open to those who call upon you.
My Lord, each lover is now alone with his beloved.
And I am alone with you.

Did Muhammad also teach that a man could have more than one wife? Yes, but only if he could support them all and love them all equally. In actual practice not many Muslims today have more than one wife.

How about those long dresses and veils that Muslim women and girls sometimes wear?

This type of clothing is intended to protect them, not to get in their way. Muslims are supposed to be modest and cover their bodies; women cover up more than men, and grownups cover up more than children. A Muslim girl doesn't want to be a sex object, so she dresses modestly and wants you to get to know her as a person.

Do girls have the same opportunities as boys in Muslim countries?

The answer to that depends on the particular place and time. Certainly there are no rules in Islam against a girl growing up to be all that she can be. (Have you ever noticed how many Muslim countries have elected women as their leaders?)

❑ *Question #3:* Muslims always stick together, don't they? If one Muslim country gets into trouble, won't all the other Muslim countries stand up for it?

◆ *Fact:* It's true that Muhammad taught all Muslims everywhere to live as brothers and sisters. Muslims of today still try to follow this noble principle. But in actual practice, Muslims are citizens of many different countries, and different countries go their different ways.

For example, *Pakistan* means land of the pure. When India got its freedom from British colonial rule in 1947, there were two mainly Muslim parts of India that insisted on having a separate country. That was the beginning of Pakistan. But in 1971 one of the two parts of this "pure" Islamic republic split off to form the new country of Bangladesh.

Another example is that Iran and Iraq are both Muslim countries; a majority of their people are even the same type of Muslims, Shi'ites. Yet, Iran and Iraq fought a long and bloody war in the 1980s. After that, Iraq started another war with Kuwait, also a Muslim country.

One more example is that all of the 150-million-plus Muslims in Indonesia are the same type of Muslims, Sunnites. Yet they are divided into four separate groups, each following a different great teacher.

☐ **Question #4:** Isn't the way of Islam only for dark-skinned people?

◆ **Fact:** The way of Islam is open to anybody who wants to follow it.

It's easy to see why Americans especially might get the wrong idea. In the years 1929–1930, an African-American started a Muslim house of worship in Detroit, saying that he had come from Makkah. Another African-American in Chicago said that he was the messenger of Allah for America. He also taught that all light-skinned people were the enemy, and that all dark-skinned people should join the Muslims and rule the world.

Other leaders who came later, such as Malcolm X, took a different view. They began to realize that dividing people according to race is not really the way of Islam. Many American Muslims of today have moved closer to the traditional teachings of Muhammad.

Where One Billion Muslims Live

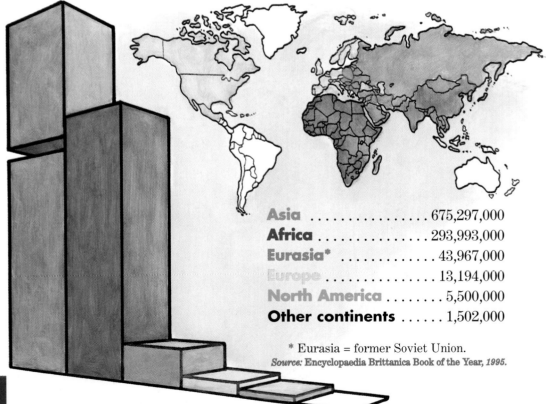

Asia	675,297,000
Africa	293,993,000
Eurasia*	43,967,000
Europe	13,194,000
North America	5,500,000
Other continents	1,502,000

* Eurasia = former Soviet Union.
Source: Encyclopaedia Brittanica Book of the Year, *1995.*

THE WAY OF ISLAM TODAY

Even after all the mistaken ideas have been cleared away, many people still feel that Islam somehow seems different from other ways of worshiping. Why do they get that feeling?

- Perhaps it's because Islam's requirements are so simple and straight-forward; they're based mainly on what human beings can do, not on shadowy beliefs or uncertain teachings.

- Perhaps it's because Islam doesn't seem to have changed as much since its beginning as other religions have.

- Perhaps it's because Muslims—even though there are many important differences among them—do seem to stick together more and do seem to be more nearly the same than followers of other faiths.

When different people use the same language in their religion, this helps to bring them closer together. Christians like to translate their holy book, the Bible, into as many languages as possible. Muslims prefer not to translate their holy book, the Qur'an; instead, they teach people to read it in Arabic.

When different people all over the world take part in the same basic kind of worship services, this also helps to bring them closer together. In 1996 a Muslim wrote, "I did the Friday prayers one week after another over a summer—at Pittsburgh, Casablanca, Karachi, Delhi, Kuala Lumpur, and Singapore. And I was always amazed at the things in common."

When different people gather from all over the world because of their religion, this does even more to bring them closer together. Every year, millions of Muslims from everywhere go as pilgrims and meet together in the holy city of Makkah.

Muslims are now the second largest group of worshipers in the world, and they're growing fast. Islam is the majority religion in 46 countries, and a strong minority in many others. Today there are more than a thousand masjids (or mosques) in the United States of America.

Whatever you yourself may think or feel about the way of Islam, you need to know about it; you need to try to understand it. For Islam plays a big part on the world scene today.

Milestones Along the Way of Islam

Being born: The first words a baby in a Muslim family hears are the traditional call to prayer, whispered into the baby's ears. The baby is named at the age of about one week; the call to prayer is repeated, and a bit of honey may be placed on the baby's tongue as a reminder of how sweet it is to pray in the Islamic way. Boys are circumcised in Islam as in Judaism, but this ceremony may be delayed till the boy is older.

Joining the worshiping community: Muslim parents begin reminding their children to pray five times a day when the children are seven years old. By the time the children are teenagers, they are expected to remember to pray on their own and are also expected to go without food during daylight hours for one month of the year.

Getting married: Muslim weddings are different in different parts of the world. The ceremony itself is usually short and simple, but there are often big parties afterward.

Dying: Dying Muslims are urged to repeat their statement of faith. Dead bodies are always washed and wrapped in cloth, but sometimes they aren't put into coffins. Muslims are buried so that they will still be facing the Kaaba in the holy city of Makkah.

Part 2

Out of Asia

5 The Way of Hinduism

What do you think of when you hear the word Hinduism?

A ❏ *A woman with a red mark in the middle of her forehead.*

B ❏ *A god with four arms, dancing inside a ring of fire.*

C ❏ *Sacred cows.*

D ❏ *India.*

All of the above answers might be correct because all of them have something to do with Hinduism. But the best answer is the last one.

It's hard to imagine India without Hindus. Both words come from the name of the *Indus,* one of the mighty rivers that curl their way around the Indian subcontinent.

To a Hindu, the whole land of India is holy—especially another of India's great rivers, the Ganges. Millions of Hindus go as pilgrims to the banks of the Ganges so they can worship as they wash in its sacred waters.

This special attachment to special places has made Hinduism slower to spread out of Asia than Christianity or Islam. Until only a few dozen years ago, most Hindus would have said, "You can't just decide to become a Hindu. The only way to become a Hindu is to be born into a Hindu family."

Nowadays that view is changing. Americans and Europeans by the tens of thousands have chosen the Hindu way of worshiping. Have you ever met a Hindu? Are you from a Hindu family yourself?

Many Americans and Europeans like to follow a particular *guru*, or one of the great teachers in the Hindu tradition who can give them *enlightenment*. Many have joined the *Hare Krishna* movement, or the International Society for Krishna Consciousness. Some people don't agree that all of these gurus and their followers are true Hindus. It's clear enough, though, that Hindu ideas and Hindu styles of worship have now spread out of Asia.

Yet the last answer to the multiple-choice question at the beginning of this chapter is still the best one. Four-fifths of all Hindus still live in just one country. But that one country has the second largest population of any country on earth. There are so many Hindus in India that Hinduism has become the third largest religion in the world today.

THE NEVER-DYING RELIGION

*H*induism is actually a name given by other people. Hindus themselves like to call their way of worshiping the never-dying religion. It is the oldest of the world's great religions. No one really knows how many thousands of years ago it got started.

Of all the great religions, Hinduism is perhaps the hardest to define or explain or even describe. It really fits in with the title of this book because there are so many different *ways* of worshiping, all of which have been called Hinduism.

No one person started this religion. Hinduism has grown and changed through hundreds and thousands of years.

■ Some people might say, "Hinduism is like a kaleidoscope." Have you ever looked down a small tube and seen a beautiful pattern of colors? You turned the tube and the pattern changed; yet it was still the same kaleidoscope. That's like Hinduism: Every time you look, you see something different about it.

■ Some people might say, "Hinduism is like an amoeba." Have you ever looked through a microscope and seen how an amoeba can make a circle around something and swallow it up? Through the long centuries, Hinduism has taken in all sorts of different beliefs and different ways of living; now all of these are parts of Hinduism.

■ Some people might say, "Hinduism is like a snowball." Have you ever watched a big snowball rolling downhill, picking up part of whatever it rolls over? The history of Hinduism has been rolling along for thousands of years; during that time it has picked up many new ideas, many new ways of worshiping.

Hinduism tries to explain who you really are. Are you the clothes you wear? the foods you eat? Are you your feet? your hands? Is even your whole body who you really are?

No. There is something inside you that is deeper and more important than anything you can see or feel. It's like your breath: You know it's there, though you don't think about it, and you don't even see it except sometimes on a cold day. Yet without that breath you would stop being a living person.

Hinduism says, "This inner part of you, this self, is really just one tiny part of the greater Self that is in everybody and everything."

Special Books for Hindus

Hinduism has more holy books than most other religions. It would take a long time even to list all of the different Hindu sacred writings, let alone to read them all. Most of these Hindu Scriptures are written in the ancient Sanskrit language.

The oldest Hindu holy books are called **Vedas**. The word *Veda* comes from the same root as *video*; it means knowledge: "Oh yes, I *see*." The Vedas are hymns to gods and goddesses. Singing or chanting hymns has been an important part of Hindu worship from ancient times till now.

These are two of the most famous Hindu holy books:

■ The **Bhagavad-Gita**, or "Song of the Lord." Some people think parts of it sound like the New Testament in the Holy Bible. Here's a sample:

> *Whoever offers to me a leaf, a flower,*
> *a fruit, or water with devotion,*
> *that offering of devotion I will accept*
> *from the pure in heart.*

■ The **Ramayana**, or adventures of the god *Vishnu* when he came to earth in the form of a young prince named *Rama*. Rama's adventures are still retold through famous dances, such as those performed under a full tropical moon on the Indonesian islands of Java and Bali.

THREE WAYS, FIVE SENSES

Hinduism has three main ways of worshiping: the way of *working*, the way of *knowing*, and the way of *loving*.

■ The way of working is the oldest way, and it's the way still followed by many people today: Obey all the rules, carry out your duties, take part in the proper ceremonies at the proper times.

■ The way of knowing doesn't mean just any kind of knowing: It means discovering the knowledge that your own innermost self really is a part of the great Self that is everywhere and in everything. (One form of the way of knowing is called *yoga*, a word that comes from the same root as *yoke*. Like an animal yoked into harness, a follower of yoga tries to bring mind and body under complete control.)

■ The way of loving usually centers on just one of the many different gods and goddesses of Hinduism. A worshiper will often repeat the name of that god or goddess. Every day the worshiper will pray to that one, trying to live a life of devotion as a faithful follower of the god or goddess.

Like followers of other religions, Hindus have many priests and many temples. Yet there's a difference. Hindu priests take care of temples and receive offerings from worshipers, but they don't necessarily lead worship services with a large group of people present. Nor is there a regular day for Hindu worship each week, like Sunday for Christians, Saturday for Jews, or Friday for Muslims.

A visitor to a Hindu temple may come at any time. Often the worshiper will come alone, bringing a gift of food or flowers and placing it before an image of a god or goddess.

Hindus like to use all of their senses when they worship:

- They *see* lighted lamps— sometimes five of them, for the five senses.

- They *hear* the ringing of a bell or the blowing of a big conch shell or the chanting of the priest.

- They *smell* the fragrance of leaves and flowers and burning incense.

- They *touch* images and other holy objects used to help them worship.

- They *taste* foods that have been blessed by being offered first to a god or goddess.

Special Days for Hindus

Special days for Hindus come not once a week but once a year— on different dates at different temples, depending on which god or goddess is mostly worshiped there.

These are two of the most common Hindu holidays:

- **Holi**, a joyous springtime festival when children get to ride in swings, eat candy, and splash colored water on everybody in sight.

- **Diwali** or **Deepavali**, a fall festival of Lights, which is celebrated much like Christmas and New Year's all rolled into one.

IMAGES OF THE ONE GREAT SELF

Why are there so many different statues and carvings in Hindu places of worship? Do Hindus worship idols? Do they think that things made of wood and stone and paint and metal can hear their prayers?

Not really. Instead, Hindus believe that the one great Self is far too great for us to understand. This greatness takes many different forms. That's why they like to use many different *images* (a better word than idols) in their worship. These images remind them of different ways of looking at the greatness of the One they worship. For example:

- An image of the god *Brahma* may have four heads. This reminds Hindu worshipers of One whose great mind can think of many different things.

- An image of the god *Ganesh* (or *Ganesha*) is part elephant, part human. This reminds Hindu worshipers of One who has great strength, like an elephant.

- An image of the god *Shiva* may have four arms. This reminds Hindu worshipers of One who can do many different things all at the same time.

■ An image of the goddess *Kali* is female, not male. This reminds Hindu worshipers that the one great Self is too great to be limited to only one sex.

A Hindu might say, "I do not worship an image. I worship a god or goddess *through* an image."

Not all Hindus like to go to temples filled with images of many gods and goddesses. More than six hundred years ago a Kashmiri woman named *Lalleswari* wrote beautiful poems, telling people about another way of worshiping—inside yourself, not with outward actions.

Two Poems of Lalleswari

Image is of stone, temple is of stone.
Above and below are all the same.
Which one of them will you worship, O foolish man?
Because inside yourself—there lies
the union of mind and soul!

Some have left their homes,
some have left their places of meditation in the forest.
What's the use of a place of meditation,
if you don't control your own mind?

Three main types of modern Hinduism center around three main gods or goddesses. Most Hindus of today are related to one of these three groups of worshipers. The marks you may have seen on someone's forehead may tell which group that particular Hindu belongs to.

Each of these three groups takes a different view of who the one great Self really is and of what it means to be a human being. Each of them focuses on one of the many different forms that the one great Self may take:

- *Vishnu*, the god who preserves life.

- *Shiva*, the god who creates life but also destroys it.

- *Devi* or *Shakti*, general names for several different goddesses who show the greatness of the One as being female rather than male.

RETURNING TO THE ONE GREAT SELF

Hindus believe that each human being has something of the one great Self inside. The great goal of life is to go back to where you came from, to become completely united again with that One.

This doesn't necessarily happen when you die. Instead, you will more than likely be born again. Your self, your soul will go into a new body, based on how good a life you have lived. You might move up the scale, becoming a person of better character, a person who understands more about life. Or, if you have lived a bad life, you might move down the scale. You might be reborn as a pig, a snake, or a bug!

This belief that human beings will be reborn is called *reincarnation*. The five letters in the middle of the word, "-*carna*-," come from a Latin word meaning body. So the word we use for this belief could just as easily have been re-embodiment.

The things you do in this life, the things that decide what will happen to you, especially in your next life, are called *karma*. Each and every thing you do will be counted and weighed . . . for good or for not-so-good.

"You Are That Self!"

Bees make honey by gathering juices from many flowering plants and trees. But when these juices are all mixed into one honey, they no longer know from what flowers they separately came.

In the same way, my child, all creatures, when they are merged in that one Self, know nothing of their past or present state.

That Self is the truth, the inner being of all.
And you, my child—you are that self!

The rivers in the east flow eastward, the rivers in the west flow westward, and all pour into the sea. Then the clouds lift them to the sky as vapor, and send them down again as rain. And when these rivers are united with the sea, they do not know whether they are this river or that.

In the same way, my child, all creatures, when they have come back from the Self, do not know where they have come from. They do not know that they are merged in that Self, and from that Self they came.

That Self is the truth, the inner being of all.
And you, my child—you are that self!

From one of the many Hindu holy books, the Chandayoga Upanishad.

Do all Hindus of today believe in reincarnation and karma?

Not necessarily. Instead, some present-day Hindus will say, "Of course, we're all a part of our past. Our roots and our family history help to decide who and what we are. And all of the things we do in this life will no doubt affect the people who will be coming along after us."

THE CASTE SYSTEM

The ancient Hindus were practical people. They decided to arrange their communities based on something everybody knows, though sometimes we don't like to admit it: People are different—not just different in their looks and likes and dislikes, but also different in what they can do and what they can't do.

At first the ancient Hindus arranged people into four classes of society, or *castes*. Here's the list as they saw it:

1. At the top of the list were priests and religious teachers, the spiritual leaders of the community.
2. Next came kings and warriors, who fought to protect the community from dangerous enemies.
3. Then came people who made things, people who bought and sold things, people who did most of the ordinary jobs in the marketplace.
4. At the bottom were people who did the jobs that were harder or dirtier, or the jobs that took less training.

Some people seemed to fall below this list of four. How about those who did the really dirty work, like cleaning up animal and human wastes? How about those who buried or burned dead bodies? How about those who tanned animal hides into leather?

People such as these gradually became known as *outcastes*. Some people called them *untouchables*, because they thought it would make you unclean even to touch such a lowly person.

Gradually the four main castes of Hinduism got divided up again into many different subgroups. Gradually this system of many levels in human society hardened like concrete into something it seemed no one could ever change. You could never leave the caste into which you were

Sacred Cows

Yes, there really are sacred cows in India. No Hindu would ever think of hurting a cow, let alone killing it. No Hindu would ever think of eating beef. (In fact, many Hindus eat no meat at all.)

Why do cows hold such a special place in the life of Hinduism?

■ Partly because of the belief that a cow might be a member of your own family who has been reborn in that form.

■ Partly because the gentle cow is a fine example of all that is good in the world of nature; she freely gives her milk to help humanity.

■ Partly because cows turn up so often in many of the ancient stories told about the god Vishnu, when he came to earth in the form of a young man named *Krishna*.

born, any more than you could leave the skin into which you were born. You mostly stayed away from people in other classes of society; you didn't sit with them or work with them or eat with them. When you got married, you had to marry someone on the same level as you.

Yet, Hindus of modern times have changed what used to be considered unchangeable. They have made many changes in their *caste system*. Gandhi, the greatest leader of twentieth-century India, taught people a new name for outcastes or untouchables: "Let's call them 'Children of God' instead," he said.

Nowadays, when people of India ride in trains and planes, there's no way to have separate seating and eating for each class of society. And when people of India go to work in a modern office or factory, there's no way to keep the castes from getting mixed together.

HINDUS—MALE AND FEMALE

Many young Hindu males take part in an important ceremony. It's a type of initiation handed down from ancient times. It may be performed while the boy is still little, or it may be put off till he has already grown to become a young adult.

The young Hindu prepares for the ceremony by shaving his head and by bathing. He dresses in special clothing and holds a wooden staff. Then, as he sits beside a sacred fire, an older man will place on his body a string woven of several cords. This reminds the young Hindu that all of life is woven together. The string will go over his left shoulder, across his chest, and under his right arm. Except when he showers or swims, he will wear it the rest of his life.

A sacred string ceremony.

Females also have a special role in Hinduism. In most Hindu homes you will find a place of worship—a room, a corner, or even just one shelf in a cabinet. There the family will keep its images of gods and goddesses. The ones who take charge of this center for family worship are usually women and girls.

Day by day the images will be gently washed with milk and water and will be honored with new clothing and sweet perfume. Day by day members of the family will bow in prayer; they will light worship lamps and bring offerings of food. This daily worship is called *puja*. On special days Hindu worshipers will also perform puja at a temple. The priest performs puja at the temple every day.

In olden times women were looked down upon in Hindu society. Girls couldn't go to school; often they were mistreated. Young widows especially had a hard time. But Hinduism has changed a lot. The worst of the old ways are long gone; the leftovers are changing fast, as girls of India get a better education. One of India's greatest leaders in modern times was a woman, Indira Gandhi.

HINDUS IN THE MODERN WORLD

Over the past two hundred years, many Hindus have become world-famous. In 1912 Rabindranath Tagore became the first writer from Asia to win the Nobel Prize for literature. But the most famous Hindu who ever lived was Mohandas K. Gandhi.

Gandhi led the fight for human freedom—first in South Africa and then in his own homeland of India. And he did all of his fighting without force. He urged his followers to take the path of nonviolence, resisting wrong without striking back. No wonder other people soon picked up Tagore's nickname for Gandhi: *Mahatma* or Great Soul.

Gandhi: "My Religion Is Hinduism"

My religion is Hinduism. For me, Hinduism is the religion of
humanity. It includes the best of all the religions I know about.
The deeper I study Hinduism, the stronger I believe that it is
as broad as the universe, and that it takes into itself all
that is good in this world.
And so I find that with Muslims I can appreciate the beauties
of Islam and sing its praises. And so at the same time with
those who follow other religions.
Still, something inside me tells me that, even though I show deep
respect for these different religions, I am all the more a Hindu.

Reworded and abridged from The Moral and Political Writings of Mahatma Gandhi,
Raghavan N. Iyer, editor, volume I. Copyright © 1986 Navajivan Trust and Raghavan N. Iyer.
Reprinted by permission of Oxford University Press.

Gandhi's great campaign finally brought freedom for India in 1947, but it also brought about his own death in 1948. The man who murdered him thought Mahatma Gandhi was being too easy in letting people of other religions go their own ways.

Gandhi's great ideas still live on. Martin Luther King, Jr., followed Gandhi's way of peace and nonviolence, as he led his fellow Americans to give full freedom to people of all races.

WHY HINDUISM IS IMPORTANT

A kaleidoscope, an amoeba, a big snowball rolling downhill: whatever Hinduism may be most like, we all need to know more about it; we need to try to understand it. The Hindu way of worshiping (or rather, the

Hindu *ways* of worshiping) is highly important in our world today. Here are four of the reasons why:

1. Hinduism is the majority religion of India, the country with the second largest number of people on earth. Some people predict that in the twenty-first century, India will even pass China and become the biggest nation in the world.

2. Hinduism is important in other countries as well. As Hindus have moved away from India, they have taken their religion with them. Hinduism is the official religion of the mountain kingdom of Nepal. People who live on the beautiful Indonesian island of Bali and also the Tenggerese tribe in the mountains of East Java follow their own forms of Hinduism. One fourth of the people of Suriname in South America are Hindus. One third of the people of Guyana and Fiji are Hindus.

3. Hinduism has also affected many people who follow other religions. For instance, ninety percent of the people of Denmark will tell you they are Christians. Yet, nearly one third of all Danish people also believe in reincarnation, as Hindus do.

4. Hinduism has a lot to teach followers of other religions about *tolerance*. This means, "You live your life and let me live mine. I won't make trouble because of your way of worshiping, so don't you bother me about my religion, either."

Milestones Along the Way of Hinduism

Being born: Even before birth, Hindus offer special prayers for both the baby and the mother. When the baby is ten or twelve days old, a naming ceremony is held. The first time the baby goes out-doors, he or she is taken to a Hindu temple. Special ceremonies also mark the first time a baby eats solid food, the first time a little boy has his hair cut, and the first time a little girl has her ears pierced.

Joining the worshiping community: On page 103 you can read about the ceremony of the sacred string.

Getting married: Hindu brides usually wear red; Hindu grooms often wear white. A wedding may last for several hours. One of the most important parts of the ceremony comes when the bride and groom walk together around a sacred fire. The groom says to the bride, "Be my friend. Let's love each other and protect each other. Let's live together for a hundred autumns!"

Dying: When a Hindu dies, the body is always cremated (burned), not buried. If possible, the ashes are scattered in running water. Sometimes American or European Hindus will send the ashes of a dead relative back to India or even take the ashes there themselves, so the ashes can be sprinkled over the holy Ganges River.

6 The Way of the Dao

A journey of a thousand miles begins with a single step.
Don't rock the boat.
A place for everything, and everything in its place.
Relax and go with the flow.
Let nature take its course.

Have you ever heard any of these old familiar sayings?

Have you ever seen a picture that looks like the illustration on page 111?

If you've ever seen or heard any of the above, then you may already have been influenced by the way of the Dao—probably without realizing it. To say the least, you've already come into contact with some Daoist ideas.

The title of this chapter actually means "The Way of the Way." *Dao* is a Chinese word for path or road or route or way. The older spelling is *Tao*, but that *T* has always been pronounced like a *D*: *DOW*.

Daoism is sometimes called "the Chinese religion." Yet Confucianism (see Chapter 9) is equally a Chinese religion. And Buddhism (see Chapter 8), though it got its start in India, also became a Chinese religion.

As a matter of fact, many Chinese through the centuries have followed all three of these out-of-Asia religions at the same time. They have blended all three of them together in many different ways.

In the middle of the twentieth century, communist rulers and teachers began trying to turn Chinese people away from believing in anything except communism (see Chapter 12). Yet, fifty years later religion was still alive and well in China, the country with far more people than any other nation on earth. For many millions of those one-and-a-quarter billion people of China, the way of the Dao is still important today.

WHAT IS THE DAO?

Just what is this Way, this Dao?

You might call it the *Way of Nature*, the way of letting things take their natural course. Familiar sayings like "Relax and go with the flow," "Doing what comes naturally," and "Let nature take its course" all seem to fit in with Daoist beliefs.

You might call it the *Way of Universal Harmony*. You know what harmony is: That's when music sounds right, when all of the notes fit together. Daoism makes a big point of saying that everything in the universe has its own proper place in relation to everything else. If anything gets out of place, then you'll hear a sour note instead of sweet harmony.

The Dao is like the channel of a river. As long as the stream flows along quietly between its banks, all is well. But what happens if the river floods?

The Dao is like people sitting in a boat. As long as you stay seated in your proper place, you can row the boat wherever you want to go. But what happens when somebody rocks the boat?

Chinese ideas about the Dao are much older than Daoism itself as a way of worshiping. Only after many centuries had passed did these ancient beliefs get put together into an organized religion.

That's one reason why some people call Daoism the Chinese religion, or even Chinese folk religion. Daoism goes deep into how the people of China think and feel and do, just as Hinduism goes deep into how the people of India think and feel and do.

WHAT ARE YANG AND YIN?

Here's another of those age-old ideas from China that later came to be a part of Daoist teachings: "Harmony happens in the universe when *yang* and *yin* are kept in balance."

Yang and yin are two kinds of energy at work in the world. They are always at work, in everything there is—sometimes more of the yang, sometimes more of the yin, but always held in balance.

The Differences Between Yang and Yin

Yang	Yin
active energy	quiet energy
daytime	nighttime
warm and dry	cool and moist
the sun	the earth
bright and clear	dark and shadowy
masculine	feminine

Look at the picture of yang and yin on page 111. The bright half of the circle is yang; the dark half is yin. But look more closely: There's a bit of dark in the yang and a bit of bright in the yin. If you cut out the yang-yin picture and made it into a pinwheel, it would whirl round and round in perfect balance . . . but the yang and the yin would still stay on opposite sides of the circle.

As far back as you can go in Chinese history, you will find the idea of the Dao and also the idea of a balance between yang and yin. For countless years these ideas have been highly important to Chinese people.

SPIRITS AND ANCESTORS

Here are two other important ideas from ancient Chinese thinking:

1. Spirits live inside everything you can see and hear and feel. Some are good spirits; some are bad. It's important to keep the good spirits on your side, so they can protect you against the bad ones. That's why Chinese people burn incense and make offerings. That's why they take gifts to temples, where priests dance and cast spells and beat on drums.

2. Every member of your family is important, even the ones who have already died. Your ancestors can still have a strong influence on you and on other members of your family living today. That's why Chinese people make a big thing out of family funerals. Then they keep on remembering their dead relatives in special ways.

Three years after death, an ancestor becomes a ghost. If living family members honor the memory of the dead, that ghost is a good ghost.

A Chinese Moon-cake.

But a forgotten or dishonored ancestor becomes a hungry ghost, wandering the earth. In Singapore today, Chinese people still keep the feast of the Hungry Ghosts. They serve *moon-cakes*: a muffin with goodies cooked inside it so that the goodies stare out at you like a full moon in a dark sky.

A THIN BUT IMPORTANT BOOK

About 500 B.C. Chinese people began to write down some of their ancient ideas and to arrange them in order. One person who is said to have done this is called *Laozi*. (The older spelling is Lao Tzu.)

A famous story says that Laozi was a government librarian who turned against both governments and libraries full of books. Driving a two-wheeled cart pulled by black oxen, he traveled far away from other people. The gatekeeper at the last gate got Laozi to write down what he believed, before he drove on toward the far West and was never heard from again.

But *Laozi* is really as much a title as a name. It simply means "The Old Master Teacher." No one knows for sure when this Laozi lived or whether there really was one particular person called by that name.

One thing is sure, though: By about 300 B.C. a thin but important book had been put into writing. Its title? *Daodejing (Tao Te Ching)*, or "The Dao and Its Power."

The Daodejing is one of the shortest of all the famous books that are special to different ways of worshiping—only about forty pages long. In 81 short poems, it makes many important statements about life on earth.

Water: Sayings from the Daodejing

Water is the softest and weakest thing on earth.
Rock is the hardest and strongest thing on earth.
Yet nothing is better than water for wearing down rock.

If you let muddy water alone,
it will clear up by itself.

Water is the most excellent thing in the world.
It helps everybody and everything.
Yet water is willing to sink down into the lowest places.
It never fights to stay up on top.

The Daodejing is full of short, loaded sentences. As you read them, you begin to understand more about the way of the Dao. Gradually you realize that this is its main theme:

"Let nature take its course. Don't fight too hard against the way things are. If you do, you might throw everything out of kilter."

Does this mean that everything that happens in the universe is good?

No, anybody can see that bad things happen, too. Yet some Daoist teachers even went so far as to say that you can never really know for sure what's good and what's bad. See the sidebar quoting "Advice from a Daoist Teacher."

Advice from a Daoist Teacher

If I slept in a wet place, I might get sick and die;
but an eel likes the wet.
If I lived in a tree, I might be nervous lest I fall;
but a monkey likes the tree.
So you see, anything might be either good or bad,
depending on who you are!

Reworded and abridged from Zhuangzi, a book of Daoist teachings.

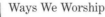

TWO VIEWS OF DAOISM

Some people say that Daoism is really two different things.

1. Daoism is a *philosophy*, a way of thinking. It's a way of looking at things, a way of trying to understand how the universe works.
2. Daoism is also a *religion*, a way of worshiping. As the long years passed, those age-old spirits that Chinese people believed to be inside everything became known as Daoist gods and demons. In temples filled with incense and images, Daoist priests told fortunes and tried to give people long life by means of magic charms.

Most Chinese people probably never worry too much about the difference between the two kinds of Daoism. Like their parents and grandparents for hundreds of generations before them, they try to keep the good spirits happy and the bad spirits far away. Sometimes they may use breathing exercises or special diets to keep everything in balance.

In their homes they set up a shelf with a little statue of the kitchen god. They write the names of their dead ancestors on small tablets and bow in reverence before them. But they will also nod wisely and quote famous philosophical sayings from the Daodejing.

More Sayings from the Daodejing

Stretch a string as far as it will go,
and you will wish you had stopped before it snapped.
Grind the edge of a blade to its very sharpest,
and you will soon find it's dull again.
Fill your house with fine things of bronze and jade,
and you will no longer be able to keep robbers away.

If you're really smart, then you will—
never try more than you can do,
never spend more than you can afford,
never think of yourself as more than you can be.

A tree too big to stretch your arms around
grew from the tiniest sprout.
A journey of a thousand miles
began with a single step.

Ruling a big country is like cooking a small fish:
Don't overdo it!

When you buy a jug, what you really care about
isn't the glass or brass or clay.
Instead, it's the empty space inside that you care about,
because you can pour useful things into it.
In the same way, don't care so much about yourself;
instead, care about your ability to receive useful knowledge.

AN OLD RELIGION WITH MODERN IDEAS

In some ways Daoism may seem to be a worn-out religion. In China, where it all began, communists have been working against Daoism for half a century. Boys and girls have been taught that the ancient Chinese

 Ways We Worship

ideas are old-fashioned superstitions. Daoist temples have been turned into museums; Daoist priests have been forced to take other jobs.

Yet, a wise man from China once wrote, "Every Chinese is really a Daoist" [Lin Tung-chi, "The Chinese Mind: Its Taoist Substratum" (*Journal of the History of Ideas*, volume 8, no. 3)]. Many people from Chinese families, now living in other countries of Asia and Europe and the Americas, still follow the way of the Dao.

For example, in Semarang, on the northern coast of the Indonesian island of Java, worshipers come from far away to burn incense and make offerings at a huge dragon-roofed temple that stretches along the base of a hill. And Chinese New Year, with its parties, parades, firecrackers, and fortune cookies, is now observed all over the world.

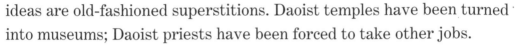

118

Chinese New Year Celebration.

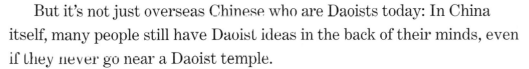

But it's not just overseas Chinese who are Daoists today: In China itself, many people still have Daoist ideas in the back of their minds, even if they never go near a Daoist temple.

So Daoism isn't a dead religion yet—not by a long shot. In fact, some of Daoism's age-old ideas seem quite up-to-date. Here's a sampling of problems in our modern world, with advice from Daoist teachings about each of them:

Arms control. Don't try to build a great nation by force of arms. Briars and thorns will grow wherever an army has camped. Hunger and rioting will grow wherever there has been a great war. Weapons may look beautiful. Yet these beautiful instruments predict a dark future, and so everybody ought to hate them. Have nothing to do with weapons, except in self-defense.

Rivalry between nations. Both great nations and small nations should learn not to be stubborn and proud. Great nations should aim to bring people together and to do people good. If they can do that without a spirit of pride, then small nations should not mind serving them.

Too much big government. The more laws there are, the more poor people there are. The more rules and regulations there are, the more thieves and robbers there are.

Ecological disasters. Don't get the idea that you can take over the universe and make it better. The universe is holy; you can't improve on it. If you try to change it too much, you'll ruin it.

The death penalty. Long ago a Chinese emperor read in the Daodejing: "If people aren't afraid of dying, then how can you frighten them with the death penalty?" That emperor had been having ten criminals executed every morning, only to find that a hundred more had committed the same crimes by evening. He stopped capital punishment, setting fines and jail terms instead. Less than a year later, the emperor felt that things were running much more smoothly in China.

HOW MANY DAOISTS ARE THERE?

How many followers of Daoism are actually left in the world today? That's hard to say.

■ One reference book says there are still about 149,300,000 "Chinese folk religionists"—149 million of them in China plus 300 thousand in the rest of the world. Probably most of these people have Confucianist or Buddhist ideas mixed in with their Daoism.

■ But another expert says that 27 percent of the people of China still follow a mixture of religions which includes Daoism. With 1,214,000,000 people living in China today, 27 percent of that huge total would number 328 million—not counting Daoists in other lands.

Any way you count them, Daoists are still important in the world of today. Isn't it interesting how many of their age-old ideas seem strangely in tune with the times in which we live?

Milestones Along the Way of the Dao

Being born: A mother will make special offerings at a Daoist temple, both before and after her baby is born. When the baby is four months old, the family makes thanksgiving offerings of peach cakes. On the baby's first birthday, he or she is shown a tray with several things on it such as a piece of money, a book, and a gardening tool. If the baby reaches first for the money, he or she will probably grow up to be rich. If it's the book, that means the baby will be smart. If it's the tool, then the baby will have to work hard, and so on.

Joining the worshiping community: Daoism has no special ceremonies when a boy or girl joins the worshiping community.

Getting married: Daoist wedding celebrations are long and complicated; few people follow all of the ceremonies today. A bride bows four times, honoring the four seasons. She is told to be a good wife, a good daughter-in-law, and a good mother. At the wedding feast her bridal veil is lifted; then the bride and groom drink from the same cup.

Dying: Daoist funerals can be very expensive. The dead person's favorite things are put into the coffin with the body. "Ghost" clothing, "ghost" money, and other "ghost" objects made of paper are burned, so they can go to the spirit world along with the dead person. You can also read about Daoist funerals and death customs on pages 112–113.

7 The Shinto Way

*Can you imagine a religion **without** any of these?*

■ *belief in a Supreme Being who is above all*

■ *holy books handed down from ancient times*

■ *written rules for right and wrong, like the Ten Commandments*

Can you imagine a religion that once was strongly connected with winning a great war, and yet, after that war was lost, the religion still lived on?

Can you imagine a religion so strongly connected with one particular country that few people of other nations have ever worshiped in that way?

You may need to use your imagination more while reading this chapter than while reading other chapters in *Ways We Worship*. If you've never lived in Japan, it may be hard for you to imagine what it's like to follow the Shinto way.

THE WAY OF THE KAMI

When you say "The Shinto Way," you're actually repeating yourself, the same as when you say "The Way of the Dao." The word *Shinto* used to be *Shen-Dao*, or the way of the *Shen*. Both *Dao* and *Shen* are Chinese words; Chinese ideas have had a lot of influence on Japan.

If you've read Chapter 6, then you already have some idea what *Dao* means. It shouldn't surprise you to learn that Shinto is more than just a religion: It's the *way* Japanese people think and feel and do—especially in relation to the things they consider to be of highest importance.

What does the *Shen* or *Shin* in *Shinto* mean? Or to use the Japanese word for it: Who or what are the *Kami*?

The Kami are spirits—spirits of power, spirits of beauty, spirits of highest rank, spirits that can influence what happens in the world.

Forces of nature are included in the Kami—wind and thunder, rivers and rocks, plants that flower and trees that bear fruit. Of course gods and goddesses are among the Kami, but human beings who have shown great strength or goodness are also included. Certainly spirits of your dead ancestors are Kami. So are the spirits that watch over you day by day, the ones some people call guardian angels.

Shinto, then, means the way of the Kami. It is the basic religion of Japan—just as Hinduism is the basic religion of India and Daoism is the basic religion of China. Through all the long centuries of Japanese history, the Shinto way has been the one thing that has kept on turning up again and again in different forms.

DESCENDANTS OF THE GODS

Shintoists believe that a god and a goddess once came down the curving bridge of heaven (the rainbow) to become husband and wife. Their children became the islands of Japan. Other children became many other gods and goddesses.

All Japanese people are considered to be descendants of one member or another of this one big family. Because of that, all Japanese people are kinfolks. But the emperor of Japan had a special ancestor.

Once upon a time, the sun goddess got angry at other Kami and hid in a cave. The whole world was covered with darkness till she could be lured out again with her own reflection in a mirror.

Then the sun goddess became troubled because the people of Japan were always arguing and fighting among themselves. So she sent her grandson down to earth with this command:

Go, my grandson, and rule over this land of reeds and rice!
Go, and may you and your children and grandchildren prosper!
May the rule of your descendants go on forever, like heaven itself!

The sun goddess gave her grandson three sacred treasures: a mirror made of bronze, a necklace made of stones, and a curving sword. The grandson then went down to Japan and started a family. Japanese people believe that his great-grandson, Jimmu Tenno, became the first human emperor of Japan in 660 B.C.

Why the Shinto Way Is Best

The true way is one and the same, everywhere;
however, only in our country is it followed correctly.
Everywhere else, people have not really understood it.
The sun goddess sends her light to the ends of heaven and earth;
every country benefits from her light, to the end of time.
However, other countries do not know how to honor her.
Our country's emperors are all descended from the sun goddess;
she has promised they will rule our nation till the end of time.
This shows that our ancient tradition is true.
Other countries say their own ways are the true ones;
yet, other countries often change their leaders and rulers.
This shows that what they say must not really be true.

Reworded and abridged from The True Tradition of the Sun Goddess *by Motoori Norinaga (1730–1801),*
one of the greatest of Shinto teachers.

Emperor Akihito, who came to the throne of Japan in 1989, is believed to be a direct descendant of Emperor Jimmu Tenno. Through all the centuries in between, each Japanese emperor at the beginning of his reign has been given a mirror, a necklace, and a sword.

THE RELIGION OF LOYALTY

An American writer (Lafcadio Hearn), after living many years in Japan with his Japanese wife, once called the Shinto way "the religion of loyalty." Here's what he meant:

■ You must be loyal, first of all, to your family, including members of it who are already dead.

■ Next, you must remember that all Japanese people are really your kinfolks. Because of this, you must be loyal to your country.

■ Above all, you must be loyal to your emperor. You must remember that he is descended from the sun goddess, and from the one she sent down to rule your land.

With this kind of loyalty, it's not too hard to understand how the Japanese people could develop a list of attitudes—unwritten at first — which they felt their noble warriors ought to have. This list is sometimes called *bushido*, or the code of the *Samurai*.

Eight Attitudes of a Noble Warrior

1. **Loyalty.** Be loyal to the emperor and to your superior officers.
2. **Gratitude.** Be thankful for all the good things you have.
3. **Courage.** Be brave enough to gladly die in battle.
4. **Justice.** Be unselfish in doing your duty.
5. **Truthfulness.** Never tell a lie to stay out of trouble.
6. **Politeness.** A strong man will be polite even to his enemies.
7. **Reserve.** Never show your feelings, no matter how strong they are.
8. **Honor.** Better to die with honor than to live without honor.

During World War II, Americans were shocked when Japanese pilots deliberately crashed their planes into American warships to make

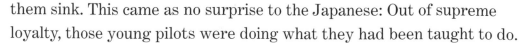

them sink. This came as no surprise to the Japanese: Out of supreme loyalty, those young pilots were doing what they had been taught to do.

In olden times, a noble Japanese warrior would always carry two swords: a long one to fight with and a short one to commit suicide with, in case he made a mistake or was defeated in battle. This type of suicide is sometimes called *harakiri*.

Loyalty of a less dramatic kind shows up in the way Japanese companies often feel about their workers, and the way Japanese workers often feel about their companies. You don't get fired if you're a member of the family. Also, you don't go on strike against your family to get higher pay.

You can see how such an attitude of family loyalty might help keep production high and prices low. That's one reason why Japan got so far ahead of other countries in industry and technology during the last half of the twentieth century.

SHINTO IN JAPANESE HISTORY

As you can see, the Shinto way and the history of Japan as a nation have always been closely tied together. Even the Japanese language blends the two. An old word for a Shinto *shrine* (or place of worship) later turns up as the word for a ruler's palace. An old word for *government* comes from the same root as the word for *worship*.

This close tie with the language and land and people of Japan has kept Shintoism alive in spite of everything. Several times in the past, it has seemed as if the Shinto religion would surely be wiped out.

More than a thousand years ago, Buddhism (see chapter 8) and Confucianism (see Chapter 9) came into Japan from China and Korea. Many Japanese liked these new teachings. The Shinto way itself took over many new ideas from both of them, especially from Buddhism. Yet it still kept its own special Japanese flavor.

For many centuries the Japanese deliberately cut themselves off from other countries. Then in the 1850s, American gunboats forced them to open up for trade. The Japanese were embarrassed to discover they were about two hundred years behind the rest of the world.

You might have expected Shintoism to be one of the old ways the Japanese left behind in their hurry to catch up. Instead, the Shinto way became stronger than ever.

During the last half of the nineteenth century and the first half of the twentieth century, Japan built up a powerful army, navy, and air force. Japanese military leaders tied their plans closely to Shintoism. "We must conquer other countries," they said. "This is only right, because after all, we are the master race, especially blessed by the sun goddess."

Japanese forces attacked Russia and Korea in the early 1900s, China in the 1930s, and the United States and its allies in the 1940s. The names of all Japanese who died in battle were written down and honored in Shinto shrines.

All of that changed when Japan lost World War II. American troops took over the islands of Japan. And on January 1, 1946, the emperor made a statement that broke the hearts of many Japanese who heard it:

O my people, what really binds us together has always been love and trust. We don't have to keep on telling ourselves old legends. I am not descended from a goddess. We Japanese are no better than other races of people; we have no special right to rule over other lands.

So, that was the end of Shintoism—right?

Wrong. In spite of everything, the Shinto way lives on. Before World

War II the Japanese government paid 16,000 Shinto priests to take care of 110,000 shrines under government control. After the war Japanese people themselves got together and made plans for taking care of their ancient places of worship. Today there are still at least 86,000 Shinto shrines being used in Japan.

In 1989 the old emperor died and a new emperor began to reign. This caused many Japanese people to take a new look at Shintoism. The Shinto way seemed to be the patriotic way, whether you took any interest in it as a religion or not.

A recent reference book says that only 3 percent of the Japanese people will tell you they are Shintoists, but 80 percent of them actually believe in the Shinto way. This would mean that more than 100 million of Japan's 127 million people are still Shintoists today.

SHINTO IN EVERYDAY LIFE

Perhaps what really keeps the Shinto way alive is the many ties it has to everyday life for ordinary people in Japan.

Most Japanese homes have a *Kami-shelf*. There you might see wood or paper tablets with names of ancestors or favorite spirits, a mirror, a stone, a small lamp, a string of beads—almost anything that might remind you of one of the Kami. (One Japanese farmer put a pair of worn-out shoes on his Kami-shelf; they had belonged to a good person who had helped him when his family was sick.) A little of the first rice cooked each day will also be placed on the Kami-shelf.

The Shinto way has always made a big thing of keeping yourself clean and pure. Special ceremonies

Shinto worshipers rinse their hands and mouths before entering a Shinto shrine.

of cleansing are an important part of the Shinto religion. Maybe that explains why the Japanese must be the cleanest people on earth. They like to bathe a lot. A Japanese home may have a hot tub big enough for the whole family at once.

Shinto festivals are times of joy for everybody. People go to family reunions, visit their friends, and eat special foods. Sometimes they parade through the streets, carrying a long brightly colored dragon mounted high on poles. The dragon may look scary, but actually it's a sign of good luck.

Festivals of the Shinto Way

January 1–3, 7 (first days of the first month): New Year's Festival.
March 3 (third day of the third month): Girls' Festival, when beautiful dolls are put out on display. See the illustration on p. 132.
May 5 (fifth day of the fifth month): Boys' Festival, when brightly colored paper fish are hung up on a pole to float like banners in the breeze—one fish for each boy in the family, arranged by age.
July 7 (seventh day of the seventh month): Summer Festival.
September 9 (ninth day of the ninth month): Festival of Chrysanthemum Flowers.

SHRINES AND MEMORIES

Each of the thousands of Shinto shrines in Japan has some special sacred object stored deep inside it. Or the shrine may be kept in memory of some special Kami, such as a former emperor.

The shrine may have behind it a mirror facing east, to reflect the rays of the sun goddess as she rises. It may have in front of it a little bridge. But you can be sure it will have a *torii* (see the symbol at the top of this page).

A torii is a simple gateway that has become the symbol of the Shinto way—like the cross for Christians or the star of David for Jews.

The most famous of all torii stands tall off the coast of an island in the Inland Sea of Japan. Its foundations are underwater at high tide. Long ago, a Shinto pilgrim carved these words:

Whether you come from the mountain or come from the sea,
when you pass under a torii, O stranger,
you will know that you have entered a new country.

A Shinto worshiper may go to a shrine to give thanks for good fortune, or to ask for help at special times in life—getting married, looking for a job, getting a promotion, retiring from work. Outside the shrine, the worshiper will first wash hands and mouth. Then he or she will clap hands, a special Japanese way of getting the attention of the Kami. Two bows before praying and making an offering, two bows afterward, and the time of worship will be over.

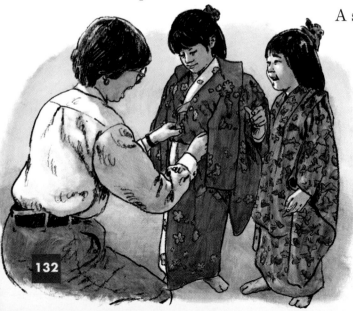

A special place for all Japanese is Mount Fuji, an extinct volcano with a famous snow-capped peak. Shinto pilgrims ring bells as they climb up its 12,388 feet, stopping to rest at ten tea-houses along the way. "May our six senses be made pure!" the pilgrims chant as they climb.

Getting ready for Girls' Festival.

Japan is one of the richest and most modern countries in today's world. Yet its people have never given up their age-old religion:

■ They still pray to the Kami—in their homes and at Shinto shrines.

■ They still follow Shinto ceremonies, for anything from a wedding to the dedication of a new skyscraper.

■ They still feel that their ancient way of worshiping helps them stay close to the beauty and power of the special land in which they live.

Milestones Along the Shinto Way

NOTE: Shinto traditions were strictly followed in Japan for hundreds of years. Not as many Japanese follow them today, but the old customs have not been forgotten.

Being born: A newborn baby is taken to a Shinto shrine, where a priest "purifies" the baby by waving a heavy stick with long paper streamers. The baby is then given a name carefully chosen to bring good luck.

Joining the worshiping community: A boy's baptism or confirmation service often takes place outdoors. Like many other Shinto ceremonies, it includes cleansing—in this case, an all-over cold splash bath as the naked boy kneels before priests who are chanting prayers.

Getting married: The bride wears a colorful kimono and a large, fancy headdress. The wedding takes place in the groom's home. The newlyweds sip rice wine from red lacquer bowls.

Dying: In Japan, Buddhist priests are considered specialists in leading funeral services. Shintoists often call on Buddhist priests when a member of the family dies. Dead ancestors are always remembered and honored.

8 The Way of the Buddha

When someone quotes an old saying or a familiar proverb, do you always agree with it? Or do you sometimes question whether those old familiar sayings are always true?

Here's a famous saying for you to test: "Every great way of worshiping is like the lengthened shadow of a great person."

True? False? Or "It depends"?

If you've been using your head while reading the first seven chapters of this book, then you know that the famous saying just quoted hasn't always turned out to be true in human history.

Yes, you could say that Judaism is like the lengthened shadow of Abraham or Moses. You could say that Christianity is like the lengthened shadow of Jesus the Christ. And you could say that Islam is like the lengthened shadow of the Prophet Muhammad.

But how about Hinduism? How about Daoism? How about Shintoism? Can you name some great person, some historical character, as the founder or focus of any one of those three great religions?

No. The old saying doesn't work for the first three out-of-Asia religions described in the second section of this book.

Starting with this chapter, the second section tells about three more out-of-Asia religions. And for these three ways of worshiping, the old saying about a "lengthened shadow" does work.

This chapter, for instance, will tell you about Prince Siddhartha Gautama, a great teacher who later became known as "the Buddha"— actually a title rather than a name, like "the Christ." The great religion he started 2,500 years ago has spread around the world, taking many different forms. Yet all forms of Buddhism today still look back to the one great Buddha. All of them could be called parts of his lengthened shadow.

Who was this historical character whose life and teachings still influence so many millions of people, even after twenty-five centuries?

PRINCE AND TEACHER

Prince Siddhartha Gautama was born about 563 B.C. His father ruled a small kingdom along what is now the border between southern Nepal and northern India. The little prince's mother died when he was a baby, but his father and his aunt took good care of him. Siddhartha lived in a different royal palace for each season of the year. He was given everything anybody could ever want . . . or so it seemed. While still a teenager he married a beautiful girl, and they had a little boy.

One day the young prince went out for a ride in his chariot and noticed a white-haired man leaning on a cane. "What's the matter with him?" Siddhartha asked his chariot driver.

"He is old," the driver replied. "But he used to be young."

The chariot passed a beggar lying beside the road; his body was covered with sores. "What's the matter with him?" Siddhartha asked again.

"He is sick," the driver replied. "But he used to be healthy."

Then they saw four men carrying another man. "What's the matter with him?" Siddhartha asked once more.

"He is dead," the driver replied. "But he used to be alive."

Back home in his palace, the prince thought about what he had seen. "I am now young, healthy, alive," he said to himself. "But someday I will be old, sick, dead. Why is life like that?" The more he thought about it, the more dissatisfied he became.

Finally one night Prince Siddhartha kissed his sleeping wife and their baby boy. With just one servant, he rode out into the dark. After crossing a river at the border of his father's land, the prince turned to his servant. "Take my horse, my sword, my jewels and fancy clothes," he said. "I'm not going to be needing them any more."

Wearing the simple yellow robe of a wandering holy man, Siddhartha started trying to find out why life is so hard, so full of hurt for everyone.

He listened to Hindu teachers, to *gurus*, to holy men who lived in caves and forests. For six long years he tried to find the answers to his questions. For days he went without eating. By making things harder for his body, he hoped to make things clearer for his mind.

Nothing seemed to help. After a time Siddhartha started eating normally again. The five holy men who had been trying to teach him were shocked; they said, "He's gone back to his old way of life." But Prince Siddhartha was still trying to find the answers.

Sitting under a fig tree in the forest, Siddhartha kept wondering why life is so hard and so full of hurt. As he was deep in thought one moonlit night, suddenly it seemed as if he had just been awakened from sleep—as if a light had just been turned on in his mind. He began to grasp what he had missed before.

"Life is hard and hurtful because we're always wanting things," the young prince said to himself. "I must stop caring so much about life. I must forget about myself. And I must try to help others understand the way to face and handle the troubles of life."

Prince Siddhartha then went in search of the five holy men who had left him earlier. He found them in northern India, at a deer park near the city of Banaras (also called Benares or Varanasi). When he told them what he had discovered, they became his first five followers.

"You are the *Buddha*, the one who has been waked up, the one on whom the light has dawned!" they cried. In the language they were speaking, *Buddha* means "the Awakened One" or "the Enlightened One."

For the rest of his long life, the Buddha traveled all over the northeastern part of India, teaching people the way he had found to face and handle the troubles of life. Many became his followers—among them, his son, his cousin, and his aunt who had taken care of him when he was little.

Not everyone liked what Buddha was teaching. One day a man in a crowd started calling the Buddha bad names. The Buddha kept quiet.

"Aren't you even going to answer me?" the man yelled.

Instead of an answer, Buddha gave him a question: "If you offer someone a gift but he won't accept it, then who does the gift belong to?"

"To the person who offered it," the man answered.

The Buddha nodded. "I do not accept the bad names you gave me, so they still belong to you. It's like someone spitting into the air: The spit falls back on your own face."

The man slunk away, ashamed. The next day he came back, asking to become one of Buddha's disciples.

Another time some of Buddha's followers told him, "People are arguing over what to believe!" The Buddha then told them a story:

Once a king invited several blind men to his palace. He had his servants lead in an elephant and asked the blind men to tell him what the elephant was like.

One man felt the head and said, "The elephant is like a great jar."

Another felt the ear and said, "The elephant is like a great fan."

Still others felt other parts of the huge beast. The one hugging its leg said the elephant was like a post, the one touching the end of its tail said the elephant was like a broom, and so on. Soon all of the blind men were quarreling.

"That's what it's like," the Buddha quietly remarked, "when each person insists, 'I know what's right, and everybody else is wrong.'"

After spending 45 years as a wandering teacher, the Buddha died peacefully with his disciples all around him. But the new way of worshiping he had started did not die.

TEACHINGS OF THE BUDDHA

What was it that the Buddha taught? What is the heart of Buddhism—even down to today, 2,500 years later?

For one thing, the Buddha taught people to think for themselves. He probably would have liked the beginning of this chapter, where you were asked to test the truth of an old familiar saying. Once Buddha said,

Don't believe anything just because somebody has told it to you. Don't even believe what your teacher says just because you respect your teacher. Instead, test everything. Then stick to whatever you find to be good and helpful.

Buddhism is sometimes called "the Middle Way." This means that Buddhism tries to keep from going to extremes in any direction. The Buddha taught,

Don't live a life filled with selfish pleasures. But don't deliberately try to make your life harder, either. There's no need for you to believe in a lot

of complicated religious teachings. But there's also no need to say that you don't believe in anything at all.

Sayings of the Buddha

Carpenters make things out of wood;
wise people make things out of themselves.

A great warrior conquers a thousand times a thousand;
even greater are people who conquer themselves.

We ourselves do wrong, or stop doing wrong;
no one can make another person pure and right.

From the Dhammapada, one of the Buddhist holy books.

One idea that often turns up in Buddhist teachings is this: The whole world has something wrong with it, and the Buddha is like a good doctor who can diagnose its symptoms. A Buddhist hymn of praise says, "You are the Great Physician for a sick and impure world."

What is the diagnosis, according to "Dr. Buddha"? What's wrong with our world? Why is it so hard to feel satisfied with things as they are?

The Buddha stated his diagnosis as *Four Noble Truths.*

1. *The Noble Truth of Suffering.* Life is hard. It hurts to be born. It hurts to grow old. It hurts to get sick and die. It hurts when you don't get everything you want. It hurts when you have to say goodbye to the people and things you love the best.

2. *The Noble Truth of the Cause of Suffering.* Life is hard and hurtful because we're always wanting things. We want what we have. We want what we don't have. Countries will even start wars with other countries, just to get what they want.

3. *The Noble Truth of the End of Suffering.* When we stop wanting things, then we'll stop hurting because we don't get them. Life will no longer be hard when we no longer want anything at all.

4. *The Noble Truth of the Way to Stop Suffering.* With this fourth truth, "Dr. Buddha" moved on from the diagnosis to the cure. He prescribed several kinds of medicine. One of them is sometimes called *Eight Steps up the Mountain*, a path that all of his followers should try to climb:

8. Right meditation

7. Right concentration

6. Right effort

5. Right work

4. Right action

3. Right speaking

2. Right purpose

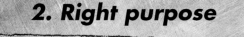

1. Right understanding

1. *Right understanding.* Understand the Four Noble Truths, as the Buddha himself did. Understand that life is hard and hurtful and that the only way to ease the pain is to stop wanting things.
2. *Right purpose.* Make it your purpose in life to want nothing for yourself, to want nothing that would hurt anyone else.
3. *Right speaking.* Say only helpful words. Don't speak in anger against anyone. Don't say anything foolish.
4. *Right action.* Be kind to everybody and everything.
5. *Right work.* Use your time and energy in ways that won't hurt anybody. Don't earn your living in any way that would make things harder for any living being.
6. *Right effort.* It's not enough just to sit back and say, "I'm a Buddhist." You must make an effort to follow the right way. You must keep your mind alert so that you can choose what is good.
7. *Right concentration.* Keep a steady focus on what is right and good and useful. Don't let your mind wander.
8. *Right meditation.* As you empty yourself of the things that cause hurt and trouble, you will become more and more able to enjoy being quiet. You will be letting peace flow into your inner self.

Meditation probably plays a bigger part in Buddhism than in any other religion. When you sit or kneel in silence, your mind may seem like the surface of a lake. All the things that have been happening to you and all the things you're thinking about are like winds stirring up waves on the lake. But as you go deeper and deeper into yourself, your mind will become more and more like the depths of the lake, where all is calm.

Does it sound hard to be a Buddhist? Actually it isn't. You don't have to go through a special ceremony like being baptized. And you don't really have to follow a lot of complicated rules. Guidelines for living as a

Buddhist can be boiled down to a short list only half as long as the Ten Commandments:

1. Try not to harm any living being.
2. Try not to take anything that doesn't belong to you.
3. Try not to use sex in any way that harms you or other people.
4. Try not to tell lies or call people bad names.
5. Try not to cloud your mind or harm your body with drugs or drink.

BUDDHISM AND HINDUISM

Buddhism got its start in India, the land of the Hindus. Hinduism was already old when Buddhism was new. How are Buddhism and Hinduism alike? How are they different?

The Buddha agreed with Hindu teachers on two important beliefs: *karma* and *reincarnation*. He taught that everything you do in life, whether good or bad, will sooner or later cause something to happen to you. He also taught that people are always wanting things; because they don't get everything they want in this life, then they have to be reborn into another life. The only way to stop the endless turning of the wheel of karma and reincarnation is to stop wanting things.

But the Buddha disagreed with Hindu gurus more than he agreed with them:

■ He didn't agree that the inner being of each person, or self or soul, is part of the one great Self that is in everything. Instead, Buddha taught that everything—we ourselves, the world around us—is in a state of constant change. How can a person have a soul if everything is always changing? "Life is like a river," the Buddha said. "Even if you stand on the bank and watch it, the water flowing by right now isn't the same water you saw five minutes ago."

An Animal Story the Buddha Told

In the high mountains a hunter once set a trap with sticky tar. A stupid, greedy monkey got one of his paws caught in the tar. He tried to push it loose with his other paw, and that one got stuck, too. Then he tried to use his hind legs to help, and then finally his nose, till the monkey was stuck in the trap five different ways.

That's like stupid human beings who are always greedy for pleasures. And what are the five ways they get stuck in the trap? Why, the five senses: seeing, hearing, smelling, tasting, and touching!

From Samyutta-Nikaya V, 148–149, one of the Buddhist holy books.

■ The Buddha didn't agree with the caste system of the Hindus, either. Instead, he deliberately tried to get all kinds of people to follow his teachings—high and low, young and old, men and women.

■ The Buddha also didn't agree with the Hindus' worship of many gods and goddesses. In fact, some people call Buddhism an *atheistic* religion, or a religion that does not believe there is a god. Buddha himself never taught *atheism*; he just didn't pay much attention to gods or goddesses. A better term to describe the Buddha is *agnostic*, a person who doesn't claim to know for sure whether there is a god or not. "What is important is you yourself," Buddha told his followers. "Each of you must find your own way to peace and happiness."

The Buddha did not only teach that you should not depend on help from any outside source such as a god or goddess. He also taught that even his own teaching as a guru could help you only so far along your way.

Like other ancient teachers in India, the Buddha used a word picture to describe his teaching: "It's like a ferryboat," he said.

India is a land of many rivers. Few of them have bridges. To get to where you want to go, you often have to ride on a ferryboat. When you gaze across a broad river, the far bank looks hazy; it's hard to tell what's over there. But as you ride across, the far bank becomes clearer and clearer while the bank you left behind becomes harder and harder to see.

"When you get there," Buddha once said to his followers, "do you then pull the ferryboat out of the water and carry it with you on the land?"

"Of course not!" his disciples snorted. "That would be foolish."

The Buddha nodded. "My teaching is like a ferryboat. When you get to the place where the light comes on for you, to the place where you awake and know and understand—then you won't need my teaching any more."

What is the final goal of the Buddhist way of worshiping? Heaven, as Christians would say? Paradise, as Muslims would say? No, Buddhists use a different word: *nirvana*. The Buddha never exactly explained nirvana, and his followers have been trying to figure it out ever since. Most descriptions only tell what nirvana is not, not what it is.

The word *nirvana* itself comes from a word that means blown out, like a candle when you puff out its flame. Does nirvana mean, then, that there is really nothing at all after death? No, Buddhism doesn't teach that, either.

Nirvana is a different kind of being, a different state of consciousness. It isn't really like heaven or paradise, because Buddhists believe you can actually go into it before you die, if in this life you stop wanting to have anything at all.

Whatever nirvana is, to Buddhists it is a condition of total peace and happiness. Maybe it isn't so strange that nirvana is hard to describe. Have you ever seen the ocean? How would you describe the ocean to someone who had never seen it?

HOW BUDDHISM SPREAD

Buddhism became the first great religion in the world whose followers deliberately tried to spread their beliefs as widely as possible. Five hundred years before there were any Christian missionaries, a thousand years before there were any Muslim missionaries, Buddhists started scattering all over Asia. They told anyone who would listen about the teachings of the Buddha.

Among the most famous Buddhist missionaries were King Asoka and his son and daughter. Asoka ruled as emperor over nearly all of India from about 269 to 237 B.C. He led nearly all of India's people to become Buddhists. He also sent Buddhist teachers to many other countries. Even King Asoka's own children, a prince and a princess, sailed to Sri Lanka as Buddhist missionaries.

Buddhism spread southeastward from India and Sri Lanka—into Myanmar, Thailand, Cambodia, Laos, Vietnam, Malaysia, and Indonesia.

The biggest Buddhist monument in the world, Borobudur, still stands today on the Indonesian island of Java. Angkor Wat, another great Buddhist temple complex in Cambodia, has been called one of the wonders of the world. Buddhism also spread northeastward—into Tibet, China, Mongolia, Korea, and Japan. But changes came over Buddhism as it spread.

Like followers of other great religions, Buddhists have divided into different groups. The three main types of Buddhism are so different from one another that they almost seem like separate ways of worshiping. Yet all three of them still look back to the Buddha for their beginnings. All three of them agree with his basic teachings, such as the Four Noble Truths and the Eight Steps up the Mountain.

The original teachings of the Buddha seemed hard for ordinary people to follow. In fact, many Buddhists felt that the only ones who could do everything he had taught them were people who separated themselves from the world: *monks* (men) and *nuns* (women). These special people broke off all ties with their own families and with anyone of the opposite sex. Monks lived together in special dormitories. Nuns did the same thing in their own centers. Day by day Buddhist monks and nuns went out carrying begging bowls to receive whatever people would be kind enough to give them.

Some Buddhists didn't like this way of following Buddha's teachings. "If the Buddha's teachings are indeed like a ferryboat," they said, "let's don't make it such a small one. Let's make a big ferryboat, so that everyone can ride!"

The biggest division of Buddhists today is called Mahayana Buddhism; the word *Mahayana* simply means the big ferryboat. Followers of this way of worshiping call the other main type of Buddhism *Hinayana*, meaning the little ferryboat. Those who feel they are sticking to the

Buddha's original teachings don't like that nickname. Instead, they call themselves *Theravada* Buddhists, meaning the way of the elders.

Besides these two major divisions, still a third kind of Buddhism (Lamaistic Buddhism) developed ages ago in the high mountains of Tibet and the high plains of Mongolia. Let's take a closer look at each of these three main types of Buddhism.

THERAVADA BUDDHISM

Theravada Buddhists feel that the most important thing is one's own individual enlightenment. For many Theravada Buddhists, the most important person is still the Buddhist monk or nun. Many young Buddhists will spend at least three months of their lives in one of those special dormitories. There they will learn the basic lessons of how to live separated from the world and all of its wants. Even the king of Thailand lived as a monk for a while when he was young.

Buddhist Holy Books

Like Jesus the Christ and the prophet Muhammad, the Buddha himself never wrote anything. For four hundred years Buddhists repeated his teachings in spoken form.

When Buddhists in Sri Lanka first began to write down what the Buddha had taught them, they wrote on palm leaves and then piled the leaves into baskets. This is why the oldest Buddhist holy books are called the **Tripitaka**, or Three Baskets.

Buddhists also have hundreds of other holy books—perhaps even more than Hindus. Each type of Buddhism has its own sacred writings in addition to the Tripitaka.

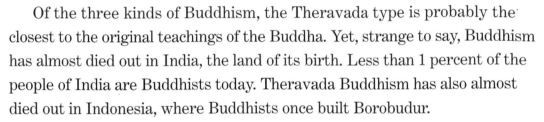

Of the three kinds of Buddhism, the Theravada type is probably the closest to the original teachings of the Buddha. Yet, strange to say, Buddhism has almost died out in India, the land of its birth. Less than 1 percent of the people of India are Buddhists today. Theravada Buddhism has also almost died out in Indonesia, where Buddhists once built Borobudur.

Theravada Buddhism is still very strong in Sri Lanka, Myanmar, Thailand, Cambodia, and Laos. With travel being as it is today, Theravada Buddhists have also moved to many other parts of the globe. About 38 percent of all the world's Buddhists are Theravada Buddhists.

MAHAYANA BUDDHISM

Mahayana Buddhists feel it's important to help as many people as possible reach enlightenment. For them, the most important person is not a monk or a nun, but rather a *bodhisattva*. This means a person in whose mind the light has dawned, as it did for the Buddha himself; notice those same three letters *b-d-h* in the words *Buddha* and *bodhisatva*. A bodhisattva does not pass on into nirvana when he or she realizes how to escape from this hard, hurtful life. Instead, the bodhisattva chooses to stay in this world, helping other people find the way of escape.

Gradually Mahayana Buddhists began to believe in many different bodhisattvas. Each one of them showed some special characteristic of the Buddha, such as his wisdom, his pity, or his sympathy for suffering humanity. The Buddha himself was a bodhisattva, because he stayed here on earth and taught people for 45 long years after becoming "the Enlightened One" while sitting under the fig tree. Through the centuries since then, many other people—men and women—have also become bodhisattvas who are worthy to be worshiped.

Some forms of Mahayana Buddhism have actually ended up with almost as many gods and goddesses as Hinduism. This seems a bit strange, for the Buddha himself said little or nothing about gods. Certainly he never taught that he himself should be worshiped as a god. Yet the Buddha was such a good and wise teacher that many people began to worship him all the same.

You can see that Mahayana Buddhism seems to show greater changes from the original teachings of Buddha than Theravada Buddhism does. In fact, Mahayana Buddhism has kept right on changing, taking many different forms. In China, Vietnam, Korea, and Japan, Buddhism

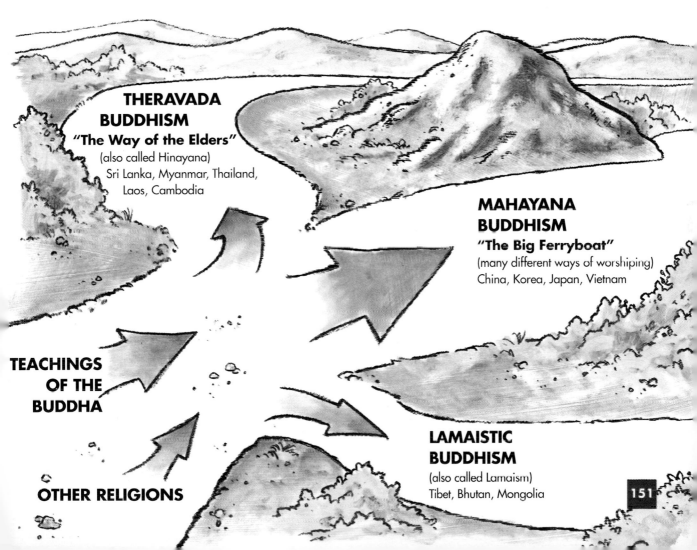

THERAVADA BUDDHISM
"The Way of the Elders"
(also called Hinayana)
Sri Lanka, Myanmar, Thailand,
Laos, Cambodia

MAHAYANA BUDDHISM
"The Big Ferryboat"
(many different ways of worshiping)
China, Korea, Japan, Vietnam

TEACHINGS OF THE BUDDHA

LAMAISTIC BUDDHISM
(also called Lamaism)
Tibet, Bhutan, Mongolia

OTHER RELIGIONS

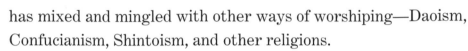

has mixed and mingled with other ways of worshiping—Daoism, Confucianism, Shintoism, and other religions.

What is the result? Today there are hundreds of different kinds of Mahayana Buddhism. One of the kinds that has become best known in America is Zen, which makes an even bigger thing of meditation than other kinds of Buddhism. One of the kinds that is strongest in Japan is Soka Gakkai, which has twenty million followers.

Mahayana Buddhists of each type have their own teachers, their own holy books, their own ways of worshiping. Yet all of them still love and respect the Buddha as the founder of their religion. About 56 percent of all the world's Buddhists are Mahayana Buddhists.

LAMAISTIC BUDDHISM

This special type of Buddhism is sometimes called simply *Lamaism*. At first the word *lama* was a title for any great religious teacher. Later it came to be the title for a Buddhist monk, especially one believed to have special powers. The most famous lama, and also the most famous Buddhist of modern times, is the *Dalai Lama*. His title means something like the monk who is an ocean of wisdom.

Like Mahayana Buddhism, Lamaistic Buddhism has taken over many ideas from other religions. Today its followers live mainly in Tibet, Bhutan, Mongolia, but also in Nepal and India.

Lamaistic Buddhists follow many ways of worshiping that may seem strange to other people—even to other Buddhists. They believe that repeating the same prayer over and over will make it more powerful. Because of this they will write a prayer on a wheel and start it turning; every turn of the wheel repeats the prayer. They will also write prayers on banners; as the banners flutter in the breeze, the prayers go up to heaven. (Can you see why some people have called this "magic Buddhism"?)

Wise Sayings of Lamaistic Buddhists

A good person is like gold, never changing;
a bad person is like a seesaw, always changing.

—————————————

If eating something sweet upsets your stomach,
how can it be right for you to eat it?
If doing something enjoyable brings you injury,
how can it be right for you to do it?

From She-rab Dong-Bu, one of the Tibetan Buddhist holy books.

Lamaistic Buddhists believe that certain great teachers, or lamas, will always be reborn when they die. They mount a big search operation to find a special baby born just at the time when an old lama has died.

In January of 1996, American newspapers told about a four-year-old boy in Seattle, Washington. After a long search, Buddhist leaders felt certain that all the signs showed this little boy was the reincarnation of a dead lama. So the child and his mother traveled all the way to Nepal, where Tibetan monks have one of their special dormitories. There the little boy began his long training as a Buddhist lama.

The Dalai Lama, like most Buddhists of the Lamaistic type, is a Tibetan. When Chinese communists took over Tibet in the 1950s, he left his homeland. Since then, he has traveled all over the world, asking for

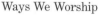
help so that his people can be free again. In 1989
the Dalai Lama won the Nobel Peace Prize.
He gave away all of his prize money to
help other Tibetans who have also had to
leave their homes.

A Prayer Quoted by the Dalai Lama

At Oslo, Norway, the Dalai Lama made a
speech when he accepted the Nobel Peace
Prize in 1989. In that speech he quoted an
old Buddhist prayer:

For as long as space endures,
and for as long as living beings remain,
until then may I, too, abide
to dispel the misery of the world.

EVERYDAY LIFE FOR BUDDHISTS

What is everyday life like for Buddhists? That depends on which kind
of Buddhists you're talking about.

Most Buddhists will have a small statue of the Buddha somewhere in
their homes. In front of it they will light candles, to remind them of the

light that dawned in Buddha's mind. They will also place flowers there, to remind them of the Buddha's teaching that all things fade and change. They will make their household shrine a pleasant place for meditation by burning sweet-smelling incense. Such worship among Buddhists is sometimes called *puja*, the same as it is among Hindus.

There have been Buddhists in America for more than a hundred years. American Buddhists like to gather at brightly decorated temples on Sundays, when most people get off from work. Often they will hold Sunday school classes for boys and girls. In their worship services, they may sing hymns, offer prayers, listen to sermons—much the same as Christians and Jews do at their houses of worship.

Buddhist holy days are different for different kinds of Buddhism. Several of their main festivals celebrate events in the life of the Buddha. Sometimes a young boy will be dressed in fine clothing, like Prince Siddhartha Gautama at first. Then he will change clothes and dress in a plain yellow robe, as the Buddha did later on.

Each night of the full moon in the lunar calendar is a special time for many Buddhists. They believe the Buddha became enlightened or awakened on a night of the full moon in the month of May. Sometimes Buddhists will stay for several days at a special dormitory or center for meditation, under the spiritual direction of a monk or nun.

Zen Buddhism got its start in China, but then it grew more in Japan. From Japan it has spread to the United States. This special type of Buddhism has had a strong influence on many forms of art and activity—landscape painting, handwriting, flower arranging, gardening, serving tea, archery, fencing (sword-fighting), and other martial arts.

How many Buddhists are there in the world today?

Two recently published source books give two widely different totals: One says 339 million. The other says 613 million!

The difference probably comes from something already mentioned more than once in this book: Many Asian people—Chinese, Koreans, Japanese—may be Buddhists while also following one or more other ways of worshiping at the same time.

Another reason why it's hard to give an exact total: Buddhism—at least in most of its forms—is not an organized religion. Many people may be Buddhists in their own minds, even though they may not say much about it.

Buddhist ideas have been mixed with Christianity to form several new religions (see Chapter 12). Buddhist ideas have also turned up in recent books and films. Popular sayings such as "Do your own thing," "Whatever turns you on," and "If it feels good, do it" got their start from Buddhist influences.

One thing is sure: Buddhists have spread all over the globe. More than a quarter million Buddhists live in Europe, and more than half a million each live in North America and South America. Wherever you may live, chances are there's a Buddhist temple not too many miles away. In number of followers, the way of the Buddha has now become the fourth largest religion in the world.

Are you yourself a follower of the Buddha? Do you know anyone who is?

Milestones Along the Way of the Buddha

Being born: In Theravada Buddhism, parents will take a newborn baby to a temple so monks can give him or her a religious name. Then a burning candle will be tilted so that drops of wax fall into a bowl of water. This is a symbol of earth, air, fire, and water all coming together.

Joining the worshiping community: There is no special Buddhist ceremony for joining the worshiping community, but there are special ceremonies when a young man becomes a monk or a young woman becomes a nun.

Getting married: At a Theravada Buddhist wedding, the monk in charge will stretch a string from a statue of the Buddha to each person present. He will chant special blessings over the string and will then cut two short pieces from it. He will tie one piece around the groom's wrist and give the groom the other piece to tie around the bride's wrist. (Monks aren't supposed to touch women.)

Dying: Monks also play an important part in Buddhist funerals. They recite special sermons and chants. In Mahayana Buddhist countries, they make a new tablet to add to the others at the place where the family honors ancestors. After the funeral, monks may also be invited to eat with the family—not just once, but many times. This is believed to help add good karma for the family member who has died.

9 The Way of Confucius

Tara and Kevin were looking down the list of musicians at a concert presented jointly by all the schools in their city. They had already spotted the names of several friends in the program folder, when they began to notice something else interesting.

"Lam, Pham, Pak, Lee, . . . ," Tara read under her breath.

". . . Kimura, Asami, Wu, Nee," Kevin continued. "Wonder why so many kids from Asian families are good in music?"

"It's not just in music," Tara whispered as members of the orchestra began taking their places on stage. "Haven't you ever noticed all those Asian names on lists of honor students?"

Maybe you've noticed the same thing Kevin and Tara did. Maybe you yourself have a family name that came from China or Korea or Vietnam or Japan. Have you ever wondered why so many American kids with Asian names seem to do so well in music and math and other studies?

One reason might be because these girls and boys have had good teachers. But another reason might go back to a good teacher who lived in Asia 2,500 years ago.

He was called Kong Fu; his pupils added -zi to the end of his name, meaning master. (Do you remember seeing that same honored title for a teacher in the name Laozi, when you read about Daoism in Chapter 6?) When people from Europe came to Asia many centuries ago, they turned Kong Fuzi into a Latin name: *Confucius*. And Confucius is the name by which that great teacher of ancient China is still remembered today.

Confucius never planned to start a religion. In fact, some people say Confucianism isn't so much a way of worshiping as it is a set of rules for living a good life. It's a little hard to separate the one thing from the other, though, because in the Chinese language the same word can be used both for *religion* and for *education*.

Whatever the way of Confucius really is, for more than two thousand years it has played a big part in making the Chinese people who they are. Because China is the largest and most important country in Asia, the way of Confucius has also helped to shape China's nearest neighbors—Vietnam, Korea, and Japan.

Who was Confucius? What did he teach? Why is he still remembered today, even by people whose families don't have Asian names?

CONFUCIUS AND HIS TEACHINGS

Confucius lived in China at the same time Prince Siddhartha, later called the Buddha, lived in India. He was born in 551 B.C. His father, a city governor, died when he was three. Confucius helped his mother feed the family by hunting and fishing. When he wasn't busy with other things, he enjoyed singing and playing tunes on a stringed instrument.

Somehow the fatherless boy managed to get a good education—no one knows exactly how. He loved to read and study. As he read, he learned that his beloved country, China, had fallen into bad times.

"Things used to be better in the olden days," young Confucius said to himself. "Children used to obey their parents. Rulers used to think about what was best for their people."

When he was grown, Confucius started working as a tax collector. But that job only made him more unhappy. He saw how other tax collectors cheated. He saw how hard ordinary people had to work to pay their taxes.

Then Confucius started a school—not a primary school, but a school for those who already knew reading and writing and other basic skills. Some people say that what Confucius started 2,500 years ago was really the first private high school or college in Chinese history, where pupils were taught to use their minds and develop their abilities instead of just to remember ancient teachings.

Physical education had its place in the school of Confucius. He taught his pupils how to shoot with bow and arrow and how to drive a chariot pulled by horses. But more important than these were lessons in music and mathematics. Most important of all were lessons about good conduct and good manners. Confucius taught that doing the right thing in every situation is more important than making high-sounding speeches.

Sayings of Confucius

I'm not one of those who claims to know a lot;
I'm only one who loves to dig up the past.
I've only passed on to others what was taught to me;
I have not made up anything of my own.
I've never gotten tired of learning,
or of teaching others what I've learned.

Do a lot of listening; leave to one side what is doubtful,
and speak carefully about the rest.
Do a lot of looking; leave to one side what isn't clear,
and act carefully about the rest.

A person of high character understands what is right;
a person of low character understands what will sell.

Whatever you don't want someone else to do to you,
then don't do that to someone else.

From Analects, *one of the Confucian classics.*

Confucius didn't teach only those who came from high or noble families. Instead, he made it a point to look for pupils with good minds, no matter how poor they might be. To rich and poor, high and low, he taught that the most important things in life are human relationships:

■ *Rulers*: Kings and governors should rule with wisdom and kindness. People should be loyal to their rulers.

■ *Parents*: Fathers and mothers should be kind to their children. Children should obey their parents.

■ *Married couples*: Husbands should take good care of their wives. Wives should honor their husbands.

■ *Children*: Older children should set a good example for younger brothers and sisters. Younger children should look up to older children.

■ *Friends*: Friends should take responsibility for the way they behave toward each other.

"If these five relationships are right," said Confucius, "then everything will be in harmony, like sweet music played in tune. But you must really mean what you say and do, not just go through the motions. You must be completely sincere."

Daoism was already old when Confucius was young. Confucius agreed with many Daoist teachings. He taught that older members of the family should always be honored, even after they are dead. But he didn't pay much attention to the world of spirits. Nor did he tell his followers to "Relax and go with the flow." Instead, he pushed them to study hard. "Learn as if you were trying to catch up with someone walking ahead of you!" urged Confucius.

A Conversation with Confucius

Once Confucius asked his disciples, "Tell me what you wish!"

Said one disciple: "I wish I had so many good things that I could lend them to my friends and never worry about them."

Said another: "I wish I would never brag about how good I am."

Then the first disciple asked, "Master, what do you wish?"

Confucius said, "I wish to comfort old people, to stay loyal to my friends, and to cherish young people."

From Analects, one of the Confucian classics.

Confucius also disagreed with Daoism in the importance he placed on good government. He taught that working for the government, if it's done right, is the highest service to humankind. He kept on hoping that the rulers of China would give him and his students high positions, so they could put his ideas into practice.

Somehow it never quite worked out that way. Confucius did get an important government job now and then, but if he found out the ruler who appointed him wasn't really sincere, then he would quit. Throughout his long life he wandered from place to place, always looking for a ruler who would do what was right, what was best for the people.

Confucius died in 479 B.C. He thought his life had been a failure. He could never have dreamed how much his teachings would affect the generations that would come after him.

CHANGES IN CONFUCIANISM

In its earliest form, the way of Confucius had no priests or ministers, no temples or services of worship. It was not like Buddhism: It had no monks or nuns giving their whole lives to their religion. It was not like Christianity: It had no missionaries carrying its teachings to other lands. It didn't even have any holy books, although the teachings of Confucius were arranged into five volumes. Four more volumes were added later on; yet all of these books were looked upon more as classic Chinese literature than as sacred Scriptures.

Even without any of the things that most religions have, the way of Confucius began to spread and develop through the centuries. Sometimes this happened because of wise men such as Mengzi (Master Meng), the greatest Confucian teacher after Confucius himself. More often it happened because rulers of China decided that Confucian teachings could make a strong foundation for their country.

Wise Words from Master Meng

People are basically born good;
yet people often fight against their own good natures.

If I feel in my heart I am wrong,
then I will stand in fear of the weakest enemy;
but if my heart tells me I am right,
then I can face an army of ten thousand.

The greatest person is the one who always remembers
what it was like to be a child.

From Mengzi, *one of the Confucian classics.*

Probably you already know that an American can't just walk in off the street and get a government job. In the early days of America, many officials were appointed only because they had voted the right way or because they were friendly with the right people. Some of these government officials did a good job; some didn't. Not till the 1880s did Americans have to start taking special tests to prove they knew enough to handle government jobs.

The Chinese had already been doing the same thing for more than two thousand years. Long ago, Chinese emperors started a system of exams based on Confucian teachings. Anybody who hoped for a government job had to pass these tests. It didn't matter how high up in society your family was: You still had to prove you were smart enough. The way to get smart was to study the Confucian classics till you nearly memorized them.

Like most ancient societies, old China was mainly ruled by men and boys. Yet women and girls had an honored place, too. No Chinese girl ever had to worry about pining away for a husband just because she didn't have a pretty face. Her parents would be sure to arrange a marriage for her anyway.

An empress of China in early times was said to be the first person to start raising silkworms. Through the long centuries, Chinese mothers and daughters kept on caring for these tiny creatures, so that from the silky cocoons they could weave the most beautiful cloth in the world.

Good Advice from Ban Zhao

If we only teach men and don't teach women, doesn't this ignore the basic relationship between men and women?
According to the rules, we should start teaching boys to read when they are eight years old. Then by the time they're fifteen, we ought to have them ready to study the classics.
Now, why shouldn't we follow the same rules for teaching girls?

From Lessons for Women, *written about 100 A.D.*

One of the greatest Chinese historians was a woman named Ban Zhao, born about fifty years after the birth of Christ. History books she wrote are still being studied today. Ban Zhao was a good Confucianist; yet she dared to question the place of women and girls in Chinese society.

Several times in its long history, Confucianism has seemed to be in danger of dying out. More than two thousand years ago, a great emperor—the same one who built the Great Wall and whose tomb is still guarded today by statues of hundreds of soldiers—decided that the way of Confucius was bad for China. He burned Confucian books, and Confucian scholars, too. Yet, not many years later Confucianism had come back stronger than ever. Confucian teachers even rewrote the lost classics from memory.

When the way of the Buddha reached China, it seemed at first a strong rival to the way of Confucius. Then many Chinese found out they could be Buddhists and Confucianists—and Daoists, too—all at the same time.

Through the long centuries people began to worship Confucius, just as they had begun to worship the Buddha.

The Great Wall of China.

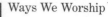

The way of Confucius gradually became a regular religion, with temples and priests. The emperor of China served as high priest, leading ceremonies year by year at the great Temple of Heaven in Beijing. Kings in Korea and Vietnam also led their people in Confucian worship services.

During the late 1800s and early 1900s, many Chinese tried to change Confucianism by bringing it up to date. But other people turned back to the old ways stronger than ever. They refused to change anything handed down from the past. This reaction against anything new is one reason why the age-old Chinese empire came crashing down in the first part of the twentieth century.

By the middle of the twentieth century, communists ruled in China. They began teaching that the way of Confucius was foolish and old-fashioned. Yet, Confucianism has never died out in the hearts and minds of Chinese people.

CONFUCIANISM TODAY

Will the way of Confucius still be a major religion in the twenty-first century? Two recent reference books say that there are only about six million Confucianists still left in the world today—far fewer than the followers of any other religion described in a separate chapter of this book.

But you mustn't forget to balance that figure of only a few million Confucianists against a fact you've already read several times: Many people in Chinese families—long ago and today, in China and in other countries—think of themselves as Confucianists, Daoists, and Buddhists, all at the same time.

One expert says that 27 percent of Mainland China's people follow Chinese traditional religions. Even if we divide that figure equally into thirds among the way of the Dao, the way of the Buddha, and the way of Confucius, we can count over a hundred million Confucianists living today in the People's Republic of China.

.Other countries add to that total. Every year on September 28, people of Hong Kong still celebrate Confucius' birthday. In Taiwan, Confucius' birthday becomes Teachers' Day, honoring all those who carry on Confucius' tradition of good teaching. Every month of June, the people of Taiwan also remember the death of a great Confucian scholar by holding their Dragon Boat Festival. One of the greatest centers of Confucian scholarship in the world today is a university in Seoul, capital city of South Korea.

Many Asian children do well in their studies.

But the strongest proof that the way of Confucius still lives today cannot be found in festivals, temples, or totals of worshipers. Instead, it shows up in the lives of girls and boys from Asian families, wherever in the world they may be living.

■ No wonder they do so well in music and in math: Confucius taught that both of these are very important.

■ No wonder they often make the best grades, and—later on—make the most money, too: Confucius taught a life-style of studying hard so you can get ahead in the world.

■ Many members of Asian families all over the world still honor their parents, still respect their teachers, and still believe in good conduct, good manners, good government. In all of these ways, people of today are following in the footsteps of Master Kong Fu, the great teacher who died 2,500 years ago—thinking he was a failure!

Milestones Along the Way of Confucius

NOTE: Confucian traditions were strictly followed in China for hundreds of years. Few Chinese follow them today, but the old customs have not been forgotten.

Being born: Babies old enough to start feeding themselves are taught to eat only with their right hands. Little ones old enough to start talking are taught to honor older members of the family by saying such things as, "May I help you?," "Bless you!," and "Have a good sleep!"

Joining the worshiping community: Sometime in his late teens a boy is presented in public, where he is ceremonially dressed in a man's cap and belt and boots and is given a new name as a grown-up. Sometime in her middle or late teens a girl's engagement is publicly announced; she, too, is given new clothing and a new name as a grown-up.

Getting married: Marriages are always arranged by older members of the family. The bride's family sends many gifts to the groom's family. On the wedding day, the groom leads the bride to his parents' house, where they then make themselves a married couple by exchanging cups of wine. After that the new couple always lives with the groom's family.

Dying: When the head of a family dies, the body is kept in a coffin for three months before burial. During all of that time special ceremonies are performed every day. After the body is buried, the dead person is mourned for another three years. During all of that time members of the family wear special clothing to show their sorrow.

10 The Sikh Way

At first Joey really wondered about the two new boys at his school. It wasn't just that they wore their hair long; other boys also chose to do that. But the younger of these two boys wore his long hair braided into a knot on the top of his head. The older boy's hair probably looked just the same if you could ever see it but he kept it tucked up inside a turban.

Luckily for Joey, Lane told him about the two new pupils before he could say or do anything he might be sorry for later.

"They're Sikhs," Lane whispered to Joey in the hall.

"Six? There's just two of 'em."

"No, Sikhs," Lane repeated. "That's their religion. And don't even think about messing with those funny hairstyles."

"Why not?" Joey wondered.

"'Cause it's supposed to have something to do with the way those new guys worship," Lane explained.

Maybe you've had Sikh friends and neighbors for such a long time that you can't ever remember wondering about them as Joey did at first. Maybe you come from a Sikh family yourself. But if you're like most people who'll be reading this book, then you may need help in understanding about the Sikh way—more help than Lane was able to give Joey.

The Sikh religion is much newer than the other great out-of-Asia religions told about in second section of this book. Maybe that's one reason why there aren't as many Sikhs as there are Hindus or Buddhists, for instance.

The word *Sikh* (pronounce it more like *seek* than *sick*) means learner or disciple in one of the ancient languages of India. Where India and Pakistan meet, five rivers run through a great plain. This is the Punjab, or Five Rivers. Three fourths of all the wheat eaten in India grows there. And there also is where *Guru* (Teacher) Nanak began teaching the Sikh way of worshiping, almost five hundred years ago.

NANAK AND OTHER GURUS

Nanak was born on April 15, 1469, in a village of the Punjab, which now lies across the border inside Pakistan. His parents were Hindus; the rulers of India at that time were Muslims. Young Nanak studied with teachers both Hindu and Muslim. Soon they were saying, "This boy has already learned everything we can teach him."

When Nanak was eleven, he was supposed to start wearing a sacred string, like other Hindu boys both long ago and today (see page 103). But Nanak said no. The beautiful words he used in explaining why not have since become a famous Sikh hymn.

From Muslims, Nanak heard that God is one. From Hindus, Nanak heard that God appears in many forms. He wondered which was right.

Why Young Nanak Wouldn't Wear the Sacred String

Take love and mercy instead of cotton;
spin them into a yarn of being content with who you are.
Tie into the yarn a clean life-style;
use truth to twist the knot.
This will make a sacred string for the soul.
Do you have such a string? Then put it on me!

From the Guru Granth Sahib, the Sikhs' holy book, and the Puratan Janamsakhi, *one of the stories of Nanak's life.*

He also wondered about the many different kinds of ceremonies and services of worship. Especially he wondered whether it was right to divide people up into castes as Hindus did.

When Nanak was a young man, he disappeared for several days; family and friends feared he was dead. When he turned up again, he explained that he had had a deep spiritual experience.

"There is only One Great Truth, One Great Reality," Nanak said. "In the sight of that One, there are no Muslims, no Hindus, no Buddhists. The One Great Reality wants us to live like brothers and sisters and to be kind to everyone."

Nanak began to wander through what is now India and Pakistan, teaching his new way of worshiping. He also journeyed as far away as Iraq and Saudi Arabia. Most people of India are Hindus; most people of Pakistan are Muslims. To the Hindus, Nanak and his followers said, "We will not bow down before many different images as you do." To the Muslims they said, "We will not bow down toward Makkah when we pray as you do."

To show that he was not against other religions, Nanak took two special friends with him on his travels. One of them was a Hindu poet he had known since they were children together. The other was a Muslim musician who played a three-stringed instrument as Nanak sang of his love for the One Great Truth.

If Nanak thought his new way of worshiping would help make friends with Hindus and Muslims, he was sadly mistaken. Through the five hundred years of their history, Sikhs have had a lot of trouble with their non-Sikh neighbors. In past centuries, the main problem was with Muslims. In more recent times, the main problem has been with Hindus.

Just before Nanak died on September 7, 1539, he named one of his faithful disciples, or *Sikhs*, to become the next Guru or teacher after him. This second Guru later chose a third Guru to follow him, and so it went for nearly two hundred years.

Things changed in 1708 when the tenth Guru said, "There will not be another human Guru like me. From now on, your teacher will be our Sikh holy book, the *Guru Granth Sahib*."

The word *Granth*, like the word *Bible*, means a collection of books. The Guru Granth Sahib is 1,430 pages long—the longest book of rhymed poetry in the world. Sikhs have taken seriously what their tenth Guru said about it.

The Sikh holy book perhaps plays a bigger part in the daily lives of Sikhs than any other holy book plays in the lives of people who follow other religions. Every Sikh home has a copy. Every Sikh child is taught to quote from it. No Sikh service of worship is ever held without a copy of the Granth being physically present. Often Sikhs will hold a nonstop ceremony of taking turns reading aloud through the entire book; it takes about 48 hours. Sikhs even greet each other day by day with words based on the Granth.

SIKHS IN WAR AND PEACE

Depending on a holy book instead of a living teacher brought about a big change in Sikhism. Another big change also came during the days of those first ten Gurus. Rulers of India did not welcome a new religion that accepted all religions. One of the Sikh Gurus was beheaded because he tried to protect Hindus. Another Guru was tortured to death. Still another saw two of his sons killed in battle; two more of his sons were bricked up in a room and deliberately starved to death because they would not change their way of worshiping.

As a result, Sikhs—who preferred to live in peace—found they had to fight to stay alive. So they started a brotherhood of soldiers. They chose special signs for their brotherhood. "We'll let our hair grow long, like Hindu holy men," said the Sikhs. "But we'll keep it neatly combed and tucked up under turbans, like the turbans Muslims wear."

Through the centuries, Sikhs became some of the finest soldiers in the world. When the British took over what is now India and Pakistan, Sikh soldiers sometimes fought for the British and sometimes fought against them. When India and Pakistan became free nations in 1947, most Sikhs chose to stay in India.

Today Sikhs make up only 2 percent of the huge population of India, but they are important people in their native land. Army officers, airline pilots, athletes on Olympic teams—these are just a few of the ways Sikhs have become well known in India.

The Golden Temple at Amritsar.

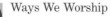

Some Sikhs think that their homeland, the Punjab, should be a separate country like India or Pakistan. In 1984 Sikhs and soldiers of India fought a terrible battle in and around the great Golden Temple at Amritsar, the holiest place in the world for Sikhs. Later that same year, two Sikh bodyguards killed Indira Gandhi, the leader of India.

But most Sikhs still like to live in peace. Partly because of troubles in India, many Sikhs have moved to other countries. In big cities of America, Europe, Asia, and Africa, you might meet Sikh doctors and dentists, Sikh teachers and taxi drivers, Sikh secretaries and store clerks. Vancouver, Canada, has now become the world's second largest Sikh city.

Three Principles Sikhs Try to Live By

1. Remember the name of the One Great Truth!
2. Earn an honest living by your own hard work!
3. Share what you have with people who have less than you do!

Most Sikhs work hard at their jobs. They also work hard at being good family members and good neighbors. Most Sikhs do not smoke, drink alcohol, or use other harmful drugs. They treat all other Sikhs like members of their own families.

Sikhs also notice the needs of their non-Sikh neighbors and reach out to help in many ways. Long before there was anything like the Red Cross or the Red Crescent, Sikhs pioneered in helping the wounded in wars, whether they were allies or enemies.

Most Sikh men and boys wear turbans. All of those long-haired males have the same family name: Singh, which means lion or lionhearted. All

Sikh women and girls have the same family name, too: Kaur, which means princess. Most females also leave their hair long, wearing scarves over their heads. Many Sikh women wear long robes or pant suits.

Most Sikhs—men and women, boys and girls—wear a steel bracelet on their right arm. The bracelet makes an unbroken circle. "That's like the One we worship," Sikhs explain. "The Force that rules the universe has no beginning and no end."

The military side of Sikhism shows up even in the symbol of their religion. Can you see those two curved swords, left and right? Can you see a third two-edged sword in the middle? (The circle, as you might guess, also reminds Sikhs that the One they worship has no beginning and no end.)

SIKHISM AND OTHER RELIGIONS

Sikhism got its start in the midst of Hinduism and Islam. How is Sikhism like each of these two much older world religions? How is it different?

Some people would say that Sikhism should have been included in the first section of this book, along with Judaism, Christianity, and Islam. They would call Sikhism a monotheistic religion—and they would be partly right. Certainly Sikhism is a *mono-* religion; the very first word in the Guru Granth Sahib, the Sikh holy book, isn't really a word: It's a numeral, the number *1*.

The problem comes in the second part of the word *monotheistic*. A *theistic* religion is a religion whose followers believe in a personal God. After you've read the first few verses of the Granth, maybe you can decide for yourself whether that which Sikhs worship—that which they consider to be of highest worth—can properly be called God.

The First Verses of the Sikhs' Holy Book

One alone there is; the name of that One is Truth, Reality.
One Great Truth is Creator of all—without fear, without hate.
One Great Reality is timeless, beyond birth and death.
Discovering that One comes through the gift of enlightenment.

From the Guru Granth Sahib, the Sikh holy book.

If worshiping "the One" were all there is to the way of Sikhism, then it would be more like Islam than Hinduism. But the Sikh way of worshiping is like Hinduism, too. Sikhs also believe in *karma* and in *reincarnation.* They believe that when they have done enough good deeds in this life, then they will not need to be reborn any more but will instead become a part of the One Great Reality.

You've already read that Sikhs have no use for the Hindus' many different images of gods and goddesses. Nor do most Sikhs have any use for the Hindus' caste system. Sikh places of worship have four doors, to show that anybody can come in, from any direction. Sikh worshipers all sit on the floor, to show that all of them are equal. They have no priests, no rabbis, no ministers in the usual meanings of these words.

One great difference between Sikhism and most other world religions—not just Hinduism and Islam but other ways of worshiping as well—is the high place given to women. Both women and men may lead Sikh services of worship. Sikh history and literature tell about many important women.

Another very important part of Sikhism is doing good to everyone. After a Sikh worship service, a community meal will be served to all who are hungry, Sikh and non-Sikh alike. Women and men will work together to prepare the food, to serve it, and then clean up afterward.

What Guru Nanak Taught About Women

It is inside women that all of us grow;
it is from women that all of us are born;
it is to women that all of us are married.
Women are the ones we choose to have as our friends,
the ones who carry on civilization,
the ones who keep everything in good order.
All the world's great people are born from women.
How, then, can we say that women are less important than men?

From the Guru Granth Sahib, the Sikh holy book.

This may sound like the sort of community service also done by followers of many different religions. Yet it isn't quite the same: Kindness and voluntary service are basic to the Sikh way of worshiping. Sometimes Sikh doctors and dentists will give free treatment, especially at festival times. In other ways as well, Sikhs try to show how much they care about their fellow human beings. At the same time, Sikhs believe that they themselves are storing up good deeds for a future reward.

Sikhs don't have one special weekly day of worship. Many Sikhs pray and sing praises every day. Others worship mainly on special days that come once a month or once a year.

Many Sikhs like to open the Guru Granth Sahib at every sunrise, when the day begins. Wherever the holy book falls open, they read the verses at the top of the left-hand page. "These are our special verses for today," Sikhs explain. They like to leave the Granth open all day long, till sunset.

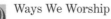

A Sikh place of worship is called a *gurudwara*, which literally means "Door of the Guru." You can always spot a gurudwara because a yellow triangle-shaped flag will be flying over it.

If you went into a gurudwara, you would take off your shoes and keep your head covered. At the front you would see a large copy of the Granth. As Sikhs come in, you would see them bow low before the holy book. Then they would sit down on the floor—men and boys on the right, women and girls on the left.

Not all Sikhs can read from the Guru Granth Sahib, because it's written in special characters. But any Sikh in the group, woman or man, might be leading the service. You would hear specially trained readers recite prayers and poems from the Granth. You would hear a lot of singing. Along with praise songs, people at the front would be beating small drums and playing small hand-pumped organs.

During a Sikh worship service, you might sniff a rich sweetness in the air. That luscious smell would be coming from a big flat dish covered with a cloth. Inside is a hot buttery, sugary pastry; later on, it will be divided up and passed around to every person there, whether a Sikh or not.

As you might expect, many Sikh holy days remember

A Sikh worship service.

the birthdays and deaths of some of their first ten Gurus. Like Hindus (see page 96), Sikhs also celebrate their own versions of *Holi* in the spring and *Diwali* or *Deepavali* in the fall.

A joyful Sikh festival comes in mid-August of every year. A sister will tie a brightly colored band around her brother's wrist, as she puts a piece of candy in his mouth. Then the brother will give his sister a present —jewelry, clothes, or money. The sister prays that her brother may have a long and happy life. The brother promises to take care of his sister, whether she marries or stays single.

In general, Sikhs don't try to lead other people to become followers of their religion. However, a Sikh teacher named Harbhajan Singh came to the United States in 1969 and started the Healthy, Happy, Holy Organization (also known as the 3HO Foundation). Through his teaching, a number of Americans have begun to worship in the Sikh way.

A Diwali celebration.

In today's world there are twenty million people who follow the Sikh way. Nineteen million of them still live in the Punjab (and other parts of India), as their grandfathers before them did. But many Sikhs have scattered to other parts of the globe. Some of them may be your friends and neighbors.

Milestones Along the Sikh Way

Being born: As soon as the mother is well enough, the whole family takes the new baby to the gurudwara. A reader gently lets a copy of the Guru Granth Sahib fall open wherever it will. Then the family chooses a name for the baby that begins with the same letter as the first letter on the left-hand side of the page.

Joining the worshiping community: A Sikh may be baptized as a baby, as a child, as a youth, or as an adult. The ceremony may be performed at the gurudwara or at home, but at least five baptized Sikhs must be present. Water is mixed with sugar in a steel bowl and stirred with a two-edged sword. Then the person joining the worshiping community (along with those who have already been baptized) drinks from the bowl. The sugar-water is also sprinkled on the eyes and hair of all baptized persons who are present.

Getting married: The bride's father places a brightly colored scarf in the groom's hand, passes it over the groom's shoulder, and puts the other end of it in the bride's hand. As hymns are sung and verses are recited from the Sikh holy book, the groom leads the bride four times around a large copy of the Guru Granth Sahib.

Dying: Sikhs accept death as a natural part of living, and so they try not to show great grief when someone dies. The body is always cremated. Many Sikhs don't pay much attention to birthdays or wedding anniversaries, but they do remember the anniversary of a loved one's death.

Part 3

In Every Continent

11 Ways Old and New

Joey's big sister is getting married. Joey is making sure he has a good supply of rice to throw at the bride and groom. When you ask him why, he shrugs his shoulders and says, "That's just what you do at weddings."

Joey might be surprised to learn how long ago the custom of throwing rice at weddings got started. He might also be surprised to learn what it used to mean. Each grain of rice is actually a tiny seed; if planted instead of thrown, it would grow a new stalk of rice. People first started throwing rice at bridal couples so they would become like a fertile field, growing many new children.

Lane likes to carry good luck charms in his pocket—a key chain with an imitation rabbit's foot, a big seed from a buckeye tree, an old blackened penny he found once on a woodland path.

Lane might be surprised to learn how long ago the people of Europe, where most of his ancestors came from, first got the idea of carrying good luck charms. It was in the late 1400s, when Portuguese sailors first landed on the coasts of Africa. People of Africa had already been carrying good luck charms for many generations before that.

Good luck that you can carry around in your pocket, customs based on old superstitions—these are some of the ways the world's oldest religions still show up in everyday life. Experts have given a special name to these oldest ways of worshiping: *primal religions*. The first part of the word *primal* means first, just as it does in *prime* minister or *primary* school. Primal religions were the first religions of people all over the world.

WHAT ARE PRIMAL RELIGIONS LIKE?

One term sometimes used to describe primal religions is *animism*. Many people, at many different places on earth and during many different times in history, have believed that things—rocks, trees, water, the sky— are actually alive and that these things have souls or spirits in them. The word *animism* comes from *anima*, the Latin word for soul or spirit.

Another term sometimes used to describe primal religions is *spiritism* or *spiritualism*. Many people, of many different places and times, have believed that the spirits of the dead can still influence people living today. They believe that certain persons can contact the spirits or even talk with them. Such a person is called a *medium*; he or she becomes the medium or means by which spirits of the dead can contact the living.

A third term sometimes used to describe primal religions is *shamanism*. A *shaman* is a religious leader believed to have special powers or special knowledge. Sometimes a shaman may also be a *medium*; he or she may pass out (or seem to) when contacting spirits of the dead.

A Chant from Africa

Those who have died are not really gone.
They are there in the deepening shadows.
They are there in the rustling trees.
They are there in the running water.
They are there in the wailing child.
Those who have died are not really under the earth:
The dead are not really dead.

Sometimes a shaman may be a *medicine man*, treating diseases of the body or mind by casting spells, doing dances, or mixing all sorts of things into a brew. (*Witch doctor* is a less polite term sometimes used for a shaman.)

Some followers of primal religions believe in many different gods and goddesses, besides believing in many different spirits. Some of them may believe in one high god over all the others. Many of these gods and goddesses are thought to be living in ordinary objects and in forces of nature—sunshine and storms, mountains and volcanoes, rivers and seas.

Followers of many primal religions believe that the way to get good things from the gods and spirits is to offer sacrifices to them. A shaman will sometimes act as priest, taking charge of whatever is placed on the altar of sacrifice. It may be animals, or crops harvested from field and orchard, or sometimes even . . . living human beings.

Followers of many primal religions believe that they can get power or control over other people. They try to do this by getting something that came from another person's body (such as hair cuttings or nail clippings) or by making a doll that looks like the person. Sometimes they may try to use their powers to make bad things happen to other people.

Most primal religions have no written Scriptures such as the Holy Bible or the Glorious Qur'an. Instead, followers of these religions may tell many kinds of *myth*. A myth is a story from olden days—especially a story explaining how things got started or why things are as they are today. (The word *myth* has also come to mean something that doesn't really exist, because most people no longer believe that these ancient stories are literally true.)

Myths were repeated from parents to children for many generations, long before anyone ever thought of writing them down. Still later, great writers sometimes reworked old myths into stories of their own—long poems such as Longfellow's "Hiawatha," short humorous explanations of "Why" and "How" in Kipling's *Just So Stories*, and many others.

WHERE HAVE PRIMAL RELIGIONS DEVELOPED?

Where on earth have primal religions developed? Where have people followed these "first" ways of worshiping?

Everywhere! Primal religions used to be the main ways of worshiping in every continent. All of the early centers of human civilization—Babylon and Assyria in Asia, Egypt in Africa, the Mayas and Incas and Aztecs in America, and all the rest—had their own primal religions.

You may have read myths once told by followers of these long-ago religions; some of them have become familiar stories in world literature. The Broadway musical *My Fair Lady* grew out of a myth of ancient Greece. Exciting books by Lloyd Alexander, Susan Cooper, and other modern authors are based on myths of ancient Wales and England.

These age-old religions have also left us great works of visual art. Painted tombs and pyramids in Egypt and in Central America, stone and jade carvings from Asia, bigger-than-lifesize masks from Africa, statues of Greek gods and goddesses—these are some of the ways primal religions have enriched our world.

DO PRIMAL RELIGIONS LIVE TODAY?

Does all of this sound like something long ago and far away?

Make no mistake here. Don't think for a minute that all primal religions are dead and gone, like the religions of ancient Greece and Rome. Some of the ancient "first" religions of humankind still live today, in at least three different ways.

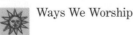

1. *Certain groups of people all over the world still follow primal religions today.*

Many Native Americans have stuck with their old religions—usually a different religion for each Indian tribe. The same thing is true for large numbers of Africans and for many tribal groups of Asia—in Indonesia, in China, in India, and in other countries as well.

A Chant of Navaho Native Americans

The mountains—I become a part of them.
The herbs, the trees—I become a part of them.
The morning mists, the clouds—I become a part of them.
The wilderness, the drops of dew—I become a part of them.

The latest issue of *World Almanac* lists more than eleven million shamanists in the world today and more than 20 million followers of "other religions" (it explains that some of these religions are forms of spiritism). Another book says that 2.7 percent of the world's population, or 144 million people, are followers of "animist/spiritist/traditional religions."

Probably even more people than these still follow primal religions today. You can find examples in every continent:

■ The world's largest local church is in Seoul, capital of South Korea. Christianity is growing fast among Koreans all over the world. Yet there are still 100,000 shamans in South Korea, most of them women. In another part of the great Asian continent, probably about half of all the people of Mongolia today worship in a way that may be described as shamanism/animism.

One person out of every five in Chad, Ghana, and Zambia follows some form of African traditional religions. In other countries of Africa such as Burkina Faso, Zimbabwe, Mozambique, and Cote d'Ivoire (Ivory Coast), it's more like one person out of every three. In Guinea-Bissau, Sierra Leone, and Liberia, it's closer to one out of every two.

In Guatemala, Central America, the ancient religion of the Mayas has taken on new life; Guatemalan tribal people seem especially attracted to this primal way of worshiping. Even in up-to-date Iceland, about 100 people are strong supporters of the old Norse religion.

Paganism is a word sometimes used for ancient ways of worshiping ancient gods and goddesses. *Pagan* used to be a sneering sort of word, as if you were looking down your nose at someone whose religion you thought wasn't as good as yours. Nowadays some 100 to 150 thousand Americans will openly tell you they are pagans. Many of them are *techno-pagans*, who light candles and burn incense while using their computers to cast spells, send out energy, and link up with fellow worshipers through one of several different pagan web sites on the Internet.

2. *Primal religions have had a big influence on all of the world's great living religions.*

All of the ways of worshiping described in this book had their beginnings in places where primal religions had already gotten there first. Leftovers from these age-old religions got mixed in—with Judaism, with Christianity, with Islam, with Buddhism, and with any other religion you can name.

Read the Jewish Scriptures. There you will find the worship of the one Lord God locked in a life-and-death struggle with primal religions. Old Testament prophets thundered out warnings against the Lord's people who sneaked away to offer sacrifices to the storm-god, Baal, or to the mother-goddess, Asherah.

The Prophet Elijah Faces a Primal Religion

How much longer will you try to have things both ways?
If the Lord is God, worship him!
But if Baal is God, worship him!

The Holy Bible: Contemporary English Version. Copyright © American Bible Society, 1995.
First Kings 18:21, quoted with permission.

Have you already read Chapters 5, 6, and 7 of this book? Then you should be able to figure out for yourself what a great influence primal religions have had on Hinduism, Daoism, and Shintoism.

Here are a few more examples of how primal religions have gotten mixed in with other ways of worshiping:

■ December 25 used to be celebrated, not as the birthday of Christ, but as the birthday of Mithra, a god in a European primal religion. December 25 was also when people noticed that the sun-god started shining a little longer each day, after the short dark days of winter.

■ Sometimes an Indonesian Muslim will ask a shaman to help cure sickness. The shaman will write a verse from the Glorious Qur'an on a scrap of paper, wash the ink off in water, and then tell the patient to drink the inky water. Nothing in Islam teaches that the Muslim holy book should ever be used in this way.

■ In 1989 a hundred-foot-tall bronze statue of the Buddha was set up in Hong Kong—"to protect the city," so people said. The Buddha never taught that he should be worshiped as a god. Nor did he ever teach that people should cast spells, turn prayer wheels, or use magic. Yet certain types of Buddhists do all of these things today.

■ Many Muslims all over the world go to pray at the graves of famous people of the past. They think their prayers are more likely to be answered because an especially good or powerful person is buried there. Other Muslims use the term "folk Islam" for these prayers; they say such prayers come from folklore, not from the Qur'an.

■ An Indonesian Christian once said, "My people are one hundred percent Christian . . . and seventy percent animist!" He said this because he knew that many of his Christian friends liked to go to shamans for help. They also liked to keep special objects in their homes or even on their persons to protect them from danger. (Belts, needles, and knives are favorite good luck charms in Indonesia.)

3. *Many "new" religions may actually be old religions; in various ways they seem to be look-alikes of primal religions.*

For example, in the last part of the twentieth century, many Americans became interested in the "New Age movement." This is not one particular religion but many different ways of looking at life.

■ Some New Age leaders say they are "channels" through which people can make contact with the spirit world. Does this sound like what a medium does in spiritism?

■ Some followers of New Age ideas believe that certain objects, such as crystals, can influence human lives. Does this sound like animism in primal religions?

■ Certain places have become centers for followers of New Age religions—Sedona in Arizona, Asheville in North Carolina, and several cities in California. Television ads invite viewers to phone in and talk with psychic network counselors. Ten thousand people in Montreal,

Canada, make their living by telling fortunes, giving advice based on contact with spirits, or helping people get in touch with forces they believe can bring them power, love, or good luck. Does this sound like a new generation of shamans?

■ Animism and spiritism are definitely still alive in religions found in several countries. Followers of these ways of worshiping may make sacrifices of eggs, chickens, pepper, goats, or rum. Sometimes they may see visions or let their bodies be taken over by spirits.

Probably the most familiar name for this type of religion is *Voodoo*, but there are many other types as well. Some experts say Voodoo got started in Benin, West Africa, about four hundred years ago; more than half of the people of Benin still follow the Voodoo religion today. Other experts say Voodoo got started in the Caribbean nation of Haiti about two hundred years ago; some 75 percent of all Haitians at least partly believe in Voodoo, although most of them will also say they are Christians.

Voodoo and other spiritist religions have spread to the United States, as people have moved from Caribbean islands. About one fourth of all Cubans believe in spiritism. Experts also say that about 50 percent of the people in the Dominican Republic are spiritists, although only 1 percent of them will come right out and tell you so.

Other religions of this type are *Obeah* in Jamaica, *Santeria* in Cuba, and *Kardecism*, *Umbanda*, and *Macumba* in Brazil. A few years ago someone counted up 14,000 spiritist centers in Brazil, with 420,000 mediums.

■ Some people say they believe in witches, or they worship Satan, the devil, or the powers of darkness and evil. Several experts who have studied different religions say that most of these ways of worshiping don't really go back to ancient times as their followers like to claim they do. Still, it does seem as if there are many new forms of primal religions these days.

Some people use a special word to describe religions like Voodoo, also religions having to do with witches or devils. The word is *occult*, which means something hidden, mysterious, or supernatural. Experts believe that 60 percent of the people of Brazil and 40 percent of the people of Iceland have something to do with the occult, even though most of these same people will say they are Christians.

■ A group of religions that may seem the strangest of all got their start on several islands in the South Pacific during and after World War II. Many of the islanders knew next to nothing about the outside world till they saw big ships and planes beginning to land. Out of those ships and planes they saw soldiers and sailors unloading all sorts of good things to eat and wear and use.

After that, the islanders began to pray for the coming of great gods or leaders who would someday arrive by ship or plane, bringing along everything they could ever want. Do you see why some people use the name "cargo cults" for these new ways of worshiping?

OLD OR NEW?

Y ou've just been reading about several relatively new religions. Do they sound strangely like old religions, like "first" religions?

Do you see how leftovers of primal religions still turn up in other ways of worshiping?

Would you have guessed before reading this chapter that primal religions still live today?

12 Ways Near and Far

Tara often watches the news on TV so she can do her homework for current events. Sometimes Tara and her dad watch the news together.

"Here's something interesting," Tara's dad said one evening as he looked up from a newsletter he was reading. "This news anchorperson thinks television ought to be reporting more about religion."

"Oh?" said Tara. "Is he some kind of a preacher as well as being an anchorperson?"

"No," her father answered. "But he does say that his beliefs have helped him develop 'the eyes to see' a spiritual side to many news stories." He turned the page of his newsletter. "The big problem, according to this person, is that 'so many people seem spooked by religion.'"

Are you one of those "many people" who "seem spooked by religion"? Does it bother you when telecasts or newspapers report religious events or tell about religious leaders? Would you have agreed or disagreed when this newsperson went on to say, "News of the soul is very much news"?

Many Americans feel that religion is something far, far away from their daily lives. They never go near a church, a temple, a masjid, or any other place of worship. They never pick up a book considered special by any way of worshiping. Yet they might be surprised to learn how near religion can come to where they live.

That's what this last chapter of *Ways We Worship* is all about: "Ways Near and Far." This chapter tries to take a look at those two comparison words "near and far" from two entirely different directions:

1. One of those two directions has already been mentioned, in the conversation between Tara and her dad about what the news anchorperson said. How *near* does religion come to your daily life? Is it near the center of who you are and what you do? Or does it seem like something *far*, far away, something out on the fringes of your life? Find answers to questions like these on pages 201–206.

2. There are many, many religions in the world today—far too many to even name them all in this book, let alone to have a separate chapter for each one. Some of these religions may seem very *near* to one another—"Nearly the same," you might say. Because of this, some people think all religions are pretty much alike. But when you look more closely, religions that seem nearly the same turn out to be *far* apart. As you read pages 206–217, you may also decide that some ways of worshiping are pretty *far* out!

NEAR OR FAR? (#1)

Many Americans like *astrology*. Each day they check the horoscope section in the morning newspaper. Each time they meet new friends, they like to ask, "Which sign of the *zodiac* were you born under?"

Astrology is something that seems very *near* to the daily lives of such Americans. They may not think of it as having anything at all to do with religion, even though some people say believing in astrology can take the place of believing in a religion. Yet astrology, when it first started, actually involved ways of worshiping. It was a part of several religions from *far* away in space and time.

More than four thousand years ago, many people living in the interior of the great continent of Asia believed that the planets and stars, the sun and moon were powerful forces in the universe. They believed that these forces could have a strong effect on human lives. That's why they started mapping out where the planets would be at any given time in relation to the sun, moon, and stars.

One among many ancient ways of worshiping that made astrology a part of religion was *Zoroastrianism*. This religion took its name from Zoroaster or Zarathushtra, a prophet who lived in Iran many centuries before the birth of Christ. (Some people think the Wise Men from the East who followed a star to find the newborn King in Bethlehem were Zoroastrians.)

By 900 years after the birth of Christ, Muslims had begun to make life hard for non-Muslims in Iran. So in 936 A.D., a group of Zoroastrians decided to move to India. How did they decide exactly when and where to move? Why, by checking out the stars and planets, of course!

In India a Zoroastrian is known as a *Parsi* or Persian, because his or her ancestors came from Persia or Iran. Today a few hundred thousand people, scattered in many different parts of the world, still follow the age-old Parsi-Zoroastrian religion. Maybe remembering them can help us also remember this important fact:

Something that seems *near* our daily lives—as near as the astrology section in this morning's newspaper, for instance—may actually have gotten its start *far*, far away, as a part of a religion from a distant place and time.

Another ancient Asian religion, *Jainism*, may seem *far*, far away from life in America today. Jainism was started by Vardhamana Mahavira, a great teacher who lived about the same time Confucius was teaching in China and Buddha was teaching in India. Somehow the history of Jainism hasn't turned out like the history of those other out-of-Asia religions. Mahavira's way of worshiping has never spread very far. There are only about four million Jains in the world today.

Yet Jainism has come *near* the lives of many people, including many Americans—a lot nearer than you might expect. One of the main teachings of Jainism is *nonviolence*—not hurting any living thing. Mahatma Gandhi, the great Hindu leader, took up the Jains' idea of nonviolence in his campaign to make India a free nation. Then Martin Luther King, Jr., the great Christian leader, learned from Gandhi to

Martin Luther King, Jr.

use nonviolence in making America a place where all races have the same rights.

Do you see why Jainism gives us another example of why it's sometimes hard to tell whether a certain way of worshiping is actually *far* or *near* in its influence on our lives?

Here's still another example: The island nation of Indonesia has the fourth largest number of people of any country in the world. Java has the largest population of any of the Indonesian islands—over a hundred million people crammed into a space the size of North Carolina or New York State. Most of these people of Java will tell you they are Muslims. But many of them—perhaps many millions of them—also follow one of several different forms of *Javanese mysticism.*

The word *mysticism* means having spiritual experiences that go beyond anything you can take in through your five senses, anything you can understand with your mind. For certain people, mysticism plays a big part in the way they worship, whether they follow the way of Judaism, the way of the Christ, the way of Islam, or some other religion. In Javanese mysticism, such mysterious spiritual experiences are especially important.

Now, all of this may seem *far*, far away from you. Yet, many young Americans have found one kind of Javanese mysticism coming very *near* to where they live. Their parents work in Indonesia—as diplomats, business executives, missionaries, and foreign aid personnel. So these American youngsters go to school in Jakarta, the huge megacity that is Indonesia's capital.

Many foreigners living on Java have been attracted to *Subud*, a type of mysticism started by a Javanese teacher born at the beginning of the twentieth century. Among these foreigners have been several teachers at the biggest international school in Jakarta. Can you see how Subud might influence the lives of teenagers—from America and other countries as well—while they are students at that school?

Subud—Far Away or Near?

Subud might be called a far-away religion that hasn't stayed all that far away. It got its start in Indonesia during the 1920s.

During the 1950s, Subud started branching out. It has now spread to sixty countries besides Indonesia. Seventy Subud centers have been started in the United States—most of them in California, but others also in New York, New Jersey, Indiana, Georgia, and South Carolina.

NO RELIGION?

The latest issue of *World Almanac* says that in the world today there are 239,111,000 *atheists,* or people who don't believe there is a God. The same source book explains that this large total also includes people who are "anti-religious (opposed to all religions)."

One of the strongest atheist or anti-religious movements ever to hit the world is *communism.* Since the middle of the twentieth century, communists in China have been teaching that all religions are a foolish waste of time.

Yet some people say communism itself is like a religion. Its "holy books" are the writings of Karl Marx and Mao Zedong. Its "worship services" are meetings of the Communist Party. Sometimes people who attend these "services" are even urged to "confess their sins" by telling all the wrong things (meaning all the anti-communist things) they've ever thought or said or done.

It's interesting to note what happened to the people of Russia, Ukraine, and Belarus during the twentieth century. For seventy years they were taught by communists to turn away from all religions . . . or would it perhaps be more accurate to say they were taught to turn away from all religions except communism?

Anyway, you can read in history books what started happening in the year 1989: Most Russian, Ukrainian, and Belarussian people decided they didn't really believe in communism after all, whether they thought of it as a religion or not. Instead, between half and three fourths of the people of these three countries have now turned back to the religion of their grandparents: Christianity.

So, what have you figured out from all of this? Do most people ever really get too *far* away from following some kind of religion? Are even atheism and other forms of anti-religion actually *nearer* to being like religions than some people may want to admit?

The newest *World Almanac* lists 924,078,000 people of the world as "nonreligious." It explains that this total includes "persons professing no religion, nonbelievers, *agnostics* [people who say we can't really know for sure whether there is a God or not], freethinkers," and people who are totally "indifferent to all religion."

It would seem correct to say that all of these hundreds of millions of people live their everyday lives *far* from any religious influence. Yet when you stop to think about it, don't most people seem to end up finding something that is *near* and dear to them, something to which they give a lot of time and attention? It may be their family; it may be their work; it may be their club or community service organization; it may be their political party; it may be their nation.

It may even be the sports team they support. Could any "worshipers" anywhere be more enthusiastic than people yelling their heads off at a ball game? On Sundays in America, do you suppose more "worshipers" gather under domes in stadiums than under steeples in churches?

No, this doesn't mean that yelling for your team is the same thing as worshiping. It's just a suggestion, a thought-starter toward a key idea: *Most people seem to find something or other which they consider to be of highest worth or value, something to which they give honor and respect*—whether they would ever think of that "something" as being their religion or not.

When you look at things from this direction, then worshiping is not so very *far* away; instead, it's *near* the lives of nearly all of us.

NEAR OR FAR? (#2)

The world of religion is full of look-alikes. Some people lump all religions together because, as they see it, most religions seem nearly the same.

If you've read carefully the first eleven chapters in this book, then you've probably noticed how *near* one religion may seem to another. But if you've really thought about what you've read, then you may have already figured out for yourself how *far* apart one religion may actually be from another—even though it may seem very near.

Here's one example of near and far, just to remind you: Sikhs, like Muslims, worship "the One." Neither of these groups of worshipers would ever think of bowing down before images of many gods and goddesses. Both of these religious groups like to read holy books written with beautiful words in ancient languages. At a glance, certain Sikhs and certain Muslims may even look alike, because they come from the same part of the world and wear the same styles of clothing.

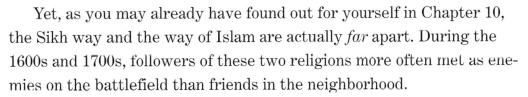

Yet, as you may already have found out for yourself in Chapter 10, the Sikh way and the way of Islam are actually *far* apart. During the 1600s and 1700s, followers of these two religions more often met as enemies on the battlefield than friends in the neighborhood.

You may remember reading that in some ways Sikhism also seems quite *near* to Hinduism. Both groups of worshipers hold several of the same basic beliefs. In fact, certain Hindus in India don't even want to recognize that there is a separate religion called Sikhism. This doesn't mean those Hindus think it's all right to worship in the Sikh way—no, indeed! Instead, they want to force their kind of Hinduism upon the Sikhs. As you might imagine, such a hard-nosed attitude has caused many Sikhs to feel *far* away from their Hindu neighbors in India.

"MIX-AND-MATCH" RELIGIONS

One reason it's hard to say whether Sikhism is *near* to or *far* from some other religions is this: Sikhism seems to be a mixture of Islam and Hinduism.

Many of the world's ways of worshiping might be called mix-and-match religions. One way of worshiping may *mix* with another, as long as the mixture seems to *match* the needs and hopes and wishes of the people doing the worshiping. The word used by experts for this kind of mixing is *syncretism*. The result, they say, is a *syncretistic* religion.

You may remember reading that Buddhism got its start in the midst of Hinduism and that Hindu ideas were later mixed in with certain forms of Buddhism. You may also remember that Daoism, Buddhism, and Confucianism have become so mixed that some people call all three of them together "the Chinese religion." Shintoism, "the Japanese religion," grew out of Daoism; later on, the Japanese also mixed in Buddhist and Confucianist ideas that seemed to match with their special way of worshiping.

Many other religions in the world today are syncretistic religions. Take the *Baha'i* religion, for instance. *Baha'ism* started in Iran during the 1800s. Today it may have as many as six million followers all over the world. Among the prophets honored in the teachings of Baha'ism are Moses (Judaism), Krishna (Hinduism), Zarathushtra (Parsi-Zoroastrianism), Buddha (Buddhism), Christ (Christianity), and Muhammad (Islam).

Two religions that started in Vietnam during the 1900s are Hoa Hao and Cao Dai. Hoa Hao, with more than a million worshipers, seems to be mainly a new form of Buddhism with a few other ideas mixed in. Cao Dai, with even more followers than Hoa Hao, seems to mix ideas from Buddhism, Daoism, Confucianism, Christianity of the Roman Catholic type, and other religions as well.

There are many such syncretistic religions, all over the world; here are a few more examples:

■ The *Religion of Three's* on the Indonesian island of Lombok mixes animism, Islam, and the type of Hinduism found on the nearby island of Bali. (Balinese religion itself seems to be a mix-and-match form of Hinduism.)

■ *Chun Do Kyo* in Korea is a religion that mixes ideas from Christianity and Confucianism.

■ Many, many new ways of worshiping in Africa seem to mix ideas from Judaism, Christianity, and African primal religions.

■ Over the past hundred years several Hindu teachers have moved to the United States and started their own ways of worshiping. Among these gurus have been Swami Vivekananda (the Vedanta Society), Krishnamurti (Theosophy), Meher Baba, Maharaj Ji (the Divine Light Mission), and Rajneesh Shree Bhagwan. Most of the religions started by these gurus are actually a mix of Hinduism with ideas from other sources.

Religions for One Race Only

Some syncretistic religions are specialty religions, intended for people of one race only. One such religion is **Rastafarianism**, started in Jamaica during the 1930s. Rastafarians like to show their way of worshiping by twisting their hair into long, tight locks.

No one should have been surprised when people whose ancestors once lived in Africa began to start their own specialty religions. For a long time, people whose ancestors once lived in Europe had been starting secret societies for their own race only. With special costumes and special ceremonies, some of these private organizations may seem very much like ways of worshiping.

A Rastafarian family.

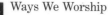

BE SURE TO CHECK IT OUT!

Do you see how important it is to check things out, to know what you really believe and why you believe it? It's especially important to get all the facts in matters of religion, because—believe it or not—*a bad choice of religion can kill you.*

- In December of 1995, sixteen wealthy members of the Swiss Order of the Solar Temple killed themselves. They were afraid the world would come to an end in the year 2000, and decided they'd rather die than live to face it. The year before, 53 other followers of this same religion in Canada and Switzerland had also committed suicide.

- In January through March of 1996, a group of rebels calling themselves The Lord's Resistance Army killed 130 people in Uganda. These Africans said they wanted to rule Uganda by the Ten Commandments as found in the Holy Bible. (The Sixth Commandment says, "Do not murder.")

- In March of 1995, members of the Aum Shinri Kyo religion sprayed nerve gas into a crowded Tokyo subway. Twelve Japanese people died; more than five thousand others were injured.

- In February of 1993, four government agents and six other people died during a shootout on a ranch in Waco, Texas. The ranch belonged to members of the Branch Davidian religion. The government agents were trying to check on why the Branch Davidians had been piling up so many weapons. Two months later, federal agents attacked again, this time with tear gas. Some of the Branch Davidians turned their guns on themselves. Others, including many children, died when the ranch caught on fire. In all, more than eighty Branch Davidians died, along with their leader, David Koresh.

■ In November of 1978 members of the Peoples Temple in Guyana opened fire on a group of American lawmakers who had flown down to check them out. Five people died, including a member of Congress from California. Later that same night, more than 900 followers of the Peoples Temple, along with their leader, Jim Jones, died when they deliberately drank fruit juice filled with poison.

You may have heard a word often used to describe "*far*-out" religious groups like these—religions that can be deadly to those who follow them. The word is *cult*. This book hasn't used that word much, because it's so hard to say exactly what it means.

As the word *cult* is used nowadays, the basic idea is a religion that seems new, strange, or different compared to other religions. As you can imagine, what seems friendly and familiar in one place might seem "new, strange, or different" in a place far away.

For example, the biggest group of Protestant Christians in the United States today is called Baptist. Nobody in America would ever think of saying that Baptists are members of a cult. For most Americans, Baptists are as *near* as the church building just around the corner.

But in other places, Baptists might seem *far* out—or at least, *far* away from any familiar type of Christianity. Baptists have been called a cult in countries as far apart as Indonesia in southeastern Asia and Bulgaria in southeastern Europe.

Instead of just talking about cults, maybe it would be better to use a more exact term. Writers of several books about religion have spoken of *destructive cults*. These are the types of religions that can destroy, the kind that can kill their own followers—and kill other people as well.

You can't always tell about a religion by its name. "Children of God" sounds great, doesn't it? Yet that's the name of a cult that has messed up

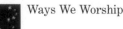

many people's lives. So how can you keep from making a bad choice? How can you be sure you'll never get hooked up with a destructive cult?

Here are some things to watch out for:

1. *Watch out when people say that they know some important secret, and they're the only ones who can teach you what is true.*

Genuine followers of any religion believe that their own way of worshiping is the right way, of course. But when people say there's important secret information that they and they alone can tell you about—be careful!

2. *Watch out when people think everybody else is The Enemy or everything that happens is part of a big plot against them.*

Strange ideas like these can cause people to do strange things. Look at what happened in Switzerland, in Canada, in Japan, in Uganda, in Guyana, and even on a ranch in Waco, Texas.

3. *Watch out when people try to get you to do things you've been taught are wrong.*

Destructive cults sometimes lead their followers—even very young followers—to have sex together, to use their bodies in harmful ways. Some cults teach their followers to steal, to do drugs, to mess up other people's places of worship. Some of them keep new members awake till all hours, drumming teachings into their ears till they're too tired to remember anything else. Use your head; why would you ever want to get mixed up with a religion that does things like these?

4. *Watch out when people seem more interested in making money than in doing good.*

Any religion may cost its followers money. Christians gladly give offerings to send missionaries. Muslims collect the cash needed to build new masjids and Islamic schools. Much the same thing is true in other ways of worshiping. But if people seem more interested in how much you have than in who you are, if they seem to want you to work hard just so you can make a lot of money for them—beware!

5. *Watch out when people don't seem to want to let you mix with anybody except their own group.*

Some destructive cults try to separate their new members from everybody else. Sometimes they may even lock up new members. They also make it a lot harder to leave their group than it was to join it in the first place. Take care!

6. *Watch out when people warn you that the end of the world is about to happen.*

Many religious people—including Jews, Christians, and Muslims—do indeed believe that the world will come to an end someday, maybe someday soon. But most of them also believe that human beings aren't smart enough to figure out exactly when that last day will come. During the late 900s, many new religions got started by predicting that the world would end exactly in the year 1000 A.D. During the 1990s, many new religions also got started by predicting that everything would go smash exactly in the year 2000 A.D.

It's good to watch out for cults—especially destructive cults. But it's not good to worry too much about them. Most really far-out religious movements don't usually attract many followers. Also, they don't usually last very long. Either they become more and more like one of the major religions, or else they gradually fade away.

That's another reason why this book has mainly tried to take a good look at just nine of the world's great religions. These two final chapters have only mentioned briefly a few of the many other ways we worship. The nine religions featured in this book have already proved that they can keep on attracting many followers over a period of many years.

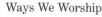

NEWER RELIGIONS

Both near and far, new religions keep on appearing. Some people say as many as one hundred different new religions get started in Japan *every year*. A recent source book lists 128,975,000 "New-Religionists" in the world today. The same book also gives a definition for what it calls "New-Religionists":

Followers of Asian Twentieth-Century new religions, new religious movements, radical new crisis religions, and non-Christian syncretistic mass religions, all founded since 1800 and most since 1945.

Sometimes the names of newer religions don't give you much help in figuring out what they're really like. Take *Iglesia ni Cristo* in the Philippines, for instance. Surely a religion with a name that means "Church of Christ" would be Christian, wouldn't it?

Don't be too sure. *Iglesia ni Cristo* has more than a million members, and these hardworking Filipino worshipers have built some of the finest church buildings you'd ever hope to see. But to become a member of *Iglesia ni Cristo*, you have to believe that Jesus the Christ wasn't really God in human form. You also have to believe that human beings don't really have a soul or spirit—something that lives on after the physical body dies. Do these sound like Christian beliefs?

Another new religion that got its start in Asia is the *Unification Church*. You may have heard the unkind nickname "Moonies" used for this group of worshipers, because their leader is a Korean named Sun Myung Moon. Many people have followed this new religion because they thought it really was a church like other churches where Jesus Christ is the central figure. Some of these same people were later shocked when Sun Myung Moon started saying that he himself is the Messiah, the Christ.

Quite a few new ways of worshiping have gotten their start on American soil. One of them goes back to the late 1800s; since 1931, its followers have been called *Jehovah's Witnesses*. This religion places great importance on teaching the Holy Bible. Because of that, many people have thought it's just another form of Christianity.

Some of these same people have been surprised later on to learn that Jehovah's Witnesses don't like to use any of the versions of the Bible used by Christians. They say the Christian Bible isn't correct in the way key words have been taken over from ancient languages. Because of this, Jehovah's Witnesses prefer to use only their own special translation of the Holy Bible.

Two other American-based religions with interesting names are the *Christian Scientists* and the *Unity School of Christianity*. If you only looked at their names, surely both of these ways of worshiping sound Christian, don't they? Yet, experts in the study of religion say that both of them have Hindu or Buddhist ideas mixed in with their Christianity.

Many people think that *Unitarian Universalists* are Christians; after all, they gather in church buildings on Sundays. Yet, followers of this way of worshiping do not believe that Jesus the Christ was any more than an outstanding human being.

One of the biggest ways of worshipping that ever had its beginnings in America is *The Church of Jesus Christ of Latter-Day Saints*. This religion was started in the early 1800s by a man in New York State who said an angel had shown him several books that were just as important as the Holy Bible. One of these sacred Scriptures is *The Book of Mormon*; that's why followers of this religion are also called Mormons. The Book of Mormon says that Native Americans are really ancient Hebrew tribes that wandered far away from Palestine.

The Mormon saga is one of the greatest success stories from American pioneer times. People living in the eastern United States made life hard for the first Mormons. They didn't like the Mormons' unusual beliefs—especially the teaching that it's all right for a man to have more than one wife. (Later on, the Latter-Day Saints stopped having such multiple marriages.) In place after place, Mormons were beaten, made fun of, run out of town, even killed sometimes.

Finally a large group of Mormons decided to move so far west that no other Americans could bother them any more. Showing great strength and courage, they followed desert trails and settled in what is now the State of Utah. Starting from scratch, they built Salt Lake City, with its great Mormon Temple and Mormon Tabernacle.

Through the years, the Latter-Day Saints have continued to show the spirit of their pioneer ancestors. Thousands of young Mormons give two years of their lives to go out two by two as missionaries. There are many millions of Mormons today, in countries all over the world.

Now, if you or your family happen to be followers of any of the newer religions just described, please don't feel that this book is trying to put down your way of worshiping.

The Temple Square in Salt Lake City.

Remember what you read in Chapter 1: This book doesn't try to show that any particular religion is either good or bad, right or wrong.

In telling about such ways of worshiping as the Unification Church, the Christian Scientists, and the Latter-Day Saints (Mormons), this chapter has been trying to show only one thing: Just because a group calls itself Christian or a church, don't jump to any conclusions. The beliefs of that group may be *near* to—or they may be *far* from—what is taught in any kind of Christian church, whether Catholic, Orthodox, or Protestant.

You could say much the same thing about other religious groups that use familiar-sounding names. Remember reading about *The Nation of Islam* on pages 14 and 86? At first glance this way of worshiping certainly seems to be Muslim. Yet Muslims in other countries can point out several reasons why they don't agree that this America-based religion is truly following Islamic teachings.

WHAT HAVE YOU LEARNED?

So now you've come to the end of this book. Have you learned some interesting things about ways other people worship?

Have you picked up some new ideas about your own way of worshiping?

Whether your own religion is old or new, whether it's near or far, whether you even think of yourself as a follower of any religion at all—maybe now you're beginning to understand more fully that the ways we worship can play a big part in making all of us who we are.

Interesting Books

After reading this book, you might like to try another book that tells about different ways of worshiping. Most books about religions are written for adults. Here are a few written for younger readers.

Bates, Sylvia, *Religions of the World.* Morristown, NJ: Silver Burdett Co./London: Macdonald Educational Ltd., 1979.

Savage, Katherine, *The Story of World Religions.* New York: Henry Z. Walck, Inc., 1966.

Ward, Hiley H., *My Friends' Beliefs: A Young Reader's Guide to World Religions.* New York: Walker and Company, 1988.

Wolcott, Leonard and Carolyn, *Religions Around the World,* illustrated by Gordon Laite. Nashville and New York: Abingdon Press, 1967.

After reading about many different ways of worshiping, maybe you'd like to try a book about just one particular religion. Here are the names of some books like that.

JUDAISM

Bates, Barbara, *Bible Festivals and Holy Days,* illustrated by Don Fields. Nashville: Broadman Press, 1968.

Cone, Molly, *The Jewish New Year,* illustrated by Jerome Snyder. New York: Thomas Y. Crowell Company, 1966.

Cone, Molly, *The Jewish Sabbath,* illustrated by Ellen Raskin. New York: Thomas Y. Crowell Company, 1966.

Domnitz, Myer, *Judaism: Religions of the World.* New York: The Bookwright Press, 1986.

Wood, Angela, *Judaism: World Religions.* New York: Thomson Learning, 1995.

CHRISTIANITY

Bainton, Roland H., *The Church of Our Fathers.* New York: Charles Scribner's Sons, revised edition, 1950. (**NOTE:** This book is quite old, but still worth looking for in libraries. It's one of the best accounts of the 2,000-year story of the way of the Christ.)

Brown, Stephen F., *Christianity: World Religions.* New York: Facts on File, Inc., 1991.

Logan, John, *Christianity: World Religions.* New York: Thomson Learning, 1995.

Martin, Nancy, *Christianity: Religions of the World*. New York: The Bookwright Press, 1986

Ward, Hiley H., *My Friends' Beliefs: A Young Reader's Guide to World Religions*. New York: Walker and Company, 1988. (**NOTE:** This book has been listed twice; it describes several religions besides Christianity, but it's especially helpful in telling about the different forms of Christianity.)

ISLAM

Edmonds, I. G., *Islam: A First Book*. New York and London: Franklin Watts, 1977.

Gordon, Matthew S., *Islam: World Religions*. New York and Oxford: Facts on File, Inc., 1991.

Knight, Khadijah, *Islam: World Religions*. New York: Thomson Learning, 1995.

Wormser, Richard, *American Islam: Growing Up Muslim in America*. New York: Walker and Company, 1994.

HINDUISM

Kadodwala, Dilip, *Hinduism: World Religions*. New York: Thomson Learning, 1995.

Wangu, Madhu Bazaz, *Hinduism: World Religions*. New York: Facts on File, Inc., 1991.

DAOISM

Hartz, Paula R., *Taoism: World Religions*. New York: Facts on File, Inc., 1993.

SHINTOISM

Earhart, H. Byron, *Japanese Religion: Unity and Diversity, 3rd ed.* Belmont, CA: Wadsworth Publishing Company, 1982. (**NOTE:** This book was written for adults, but you might like to read some of it anyway.)

Seeger, Elizabeth, *Eastern Religions*. New York: Thomas Y. Crowell Company, 1973. (**NOTE:** This book has long chapters on Japanese and Chinese religions.)

BUDDHISM

Edmonds, I. G., *Buddhism: A First Book*. New York and London: Franklin Watts, 1978.

Hewitt, Catherine, *Buddhism: World Religions*. New York: Thomson Learning, 1995.

Snelling, John, *Buddhism: Religions of the World*. New York: The Bookwright Press, 1986.

Wangu, Madhu Bazaz, *Buddhism: World Religions*. New York: Facts on File, Inc., 1993.

CONFUCIANISM

Hoobler, Thomas and Dorothy, *Confucianism: World Religions*. New York and Oxford: Facts on File, 1993.

SIKHISM

Aggarwal, Manju, Harjeet Singh Lal, and Chris Fairclough, *I Am a Sikh*. London, New York, Sydney, and Toronto: Franklin Watts, Inc., 1985.

Kaur-Singh, Kanwaljit, *Sikhism: World Religions*. New York: Thomson Learning, 1995.

Singh, Nikky-Guninder Kaur, *Sikhism: World Religions*. New York and Oxford: Facts On File, Inc., 1993.

OTHER RELIGIONS

Cohen, Daniel, *Cults*. Brookfield, CT: The Millbrook Press, 1994.

Miller, Maryann, *Coping with Cults*. New York: Rosen Publishing Group, Inc., 1990.

Starkes, M. Thomas, *Confronting Popular Cults*. Nashville: Broadman Press, 1972.

Stevens, Sarah, *The Facts About Cults*. New York: Crestwood House, Macmillan Publishing Company, 1992.

Even books written for adults may be interesting to younger readers if they have lots of photographs, drawings, and maps. You might like to take a look at some of these books about different ways of worshiping.

Beaver, R. Pierce, et al., editors, *Eerdmans' Handbook to the World's Religions*. Grand Rapids, MI: William B. Eerdmans Publishing Company, 1982.

Clarke, Peter B., editor, *The World's Religions: Understanding the Living Faiths*. Pleasantville, NY, and Montreal: The Reader's Digest Association, Inc., 1993.

Forman, Henry James, and Roland Gammon, *Truth Is One: The Story of the World's Great Living Religions in Pictures and Text*. New York and Evanston, IL: Harper & Row, Publishers, 1954.

Makhlouf, Georgia, and Walter O. Moeller, *The Human Story: The Rise of Major Religions,* illustrated by Michael Welply. Englewood Cliffs, NJ: Silver Burdett Press, 1986, 1988.

Severy, Merle, et al., editors, *Great Religions of the World*. Washington: National Geographic Society, 1971, 1978.

Smart, Ninian, *The Long Search*. Boston and Toronto: Little, Brown and Company, 1977.

Smith, Huston, *The Illustrated World's Religions: A Guide to Our Wisdom Traditions*. New York and San Francisco: HarperCollins, 1991, 1994.

Welles, Sam, et al., editor, *The World's Great Religions*. New York: Time Incorporated, 1957.

Important Words

*When a word is in **heavy dark** print, it has its own definition in this section.*

Abraham (AY-brah-ham) One of the founding fathers of Judaism (see pp. 14, 25–26); also honored by Christians (see p. 14) and by Muslims (see pp. 15, 73, 75).

Acts, Acts of the Apostles (AKTZ of the uh-POSS-l'z) History of the beginning of Christianity, written by **Luke** (a Greek doctor); part of the **New Testament** in **the Holy Bible** (see pp. 6, 48).

A.D. Abbreviation for *Anno Domini*, meaning Year of Our Lord (see pp. 12, 72).

Adventist (ADD-vent-ist) Name used by several Christian denominations of the Protestant type (see p. 56).

agnostic (ag-NAHS-tick), ***agnosticism*** (ag-NAHS-tuh-siz'm) Belief that there is no way to know whether there is a god or not (see pp. 145, 205).

A.H. Abbreviation used in the Muslim calendar, counting years after the **hijra** or **hegira** (see p. 72).

Ali (AH-lee) Cousin, son-in-law, and first follower of Muhammad, especially honored by Muslims of the **Shi'ite** type (see p. 82); see also **imam**.

Allah (AH-lah) Arabic words meaning *the* God, used mainly by Muslims (see pp. 67, 68, 69–70, 77–79, 86) but also by some Christians (see p. 68).

Alawites (AH-lah-weets) Type of Muslims (see p. 83).

American Muslims (MOOS-limz) Certain American **Muslims** are considered true Muslims by some Muslims in other countries, but certain other American Muslims are not (see pp. 14, 86, 217); see also **The Nation of Islam**.

Amish (AH-mish) Name used by several Christian denominations of the Protestant type (see p. 56).

Amritsar (om-RIT-sur) City in India, location of the holiest place in the world for Sikhs (see pp. 177–178).

ancestors (ANN-ses-turz) Older members of the family who have already died. They are especially important in Daoism (see pp. 112–113, 116), Shintoism (see pp.127, 130, 133), Buddhism (see p. 157), and other religions.

Anglican (ANG-li-kun) Christian denomination of the Protestant type (see p. 56).

Anglo-Catholic (ANG-glow KATH-uh-lick) Christian denomination of the Catholic type (see p. 54).

animism (ANN-uh-miz'm) Belief that things—such as rocks, trees, water, the sky—have souls or spirits in them (see pp. 188, 192, 195).

anointed (uh-NOYN-tid) Placing oil or ointment on a person's forehead to show how special he or she is (see pp. 30, 42, 47); also used as a figure of speech for being touched by the power of God's **Holy Spirit** (see pp. 58–59).

anti-Semitism (an-tie-SEM-uh-tiz'm) Anti-Jewish feelings and actions (see pp. 31–34, 37).

apostles (uh-POSS-l'z) Sent-out ones; a name Jesus gave to his first **disciples** (see p. 48).

Armenian Apostolic (ar-MEE-ni-yan ap-poss-TAH-lick) Christian denomination of the Orthodox type (see p. 54).

Asoka (uh-SO-kah) King or emperor in India who did a lot to spread Buddhism (see p. 147).

Assemblies (uh-SEM-blihz) *of God* Christian denomination of the Protestant type (see p. 56).

astrology (uh-STRAH-luh-jih) Belief that the relative positions of the planets, sun, moon, and stars can affect human lives (see pp. 201–202).

atheism (AY-thih-iz'm), **atheistic religion** (ay-thih-ISS-tick) Belief that there is no god (see pp. 145, 204–205).

atonement (uh-TONE-ment) Act that makes a worshiper feel *at-one* with God again, not separated from God by sin and guilt (see pp. 24–25, 47).

Aum Shinri Kyo (ah-oom shin-ree KYO) **Destructive cult** in twentieth-century Japan (see p. 210).

awakening (uh-WAY-kun-ing) In Buddhism, means the same as **enlightenment** (see pp. 138, 146, 149, 150).

Baha'i (BAH-hi), **Baha'ism** (BAH-hi-iz'm) **Syncretistic religion** started in Iran in the 1800s (see p. 208).

Banaras (bah-NAH-rahs) City in northern India where the Buddha first began teaching; same as Benares or Varanasi (see p. 138).

Ban Zhao (ban ZHAH-o) Woman follower of Confucianism who became one of the greatest Chinese historians (see pp. 166–167).

baptism (BAP-tiz'm) Ceremony using water, performed when someone joins the worshiping community; several different forms of baptism are practiced by different kinds of Christians (see pp. 51–52, 65), by Sikhs (see p. 184), and (at least in the past) by Shintoists (see p. 133).

Baptist (BAP-tist) Name used by several Christian denominations of the Protestant type (see pp. 56, 63, 211).

bar mitzvah (bar-MITZ-vah) Ceremony when a Jewish boy joins the worshiping community (see pp. 36–37).

bat mitzvah (baht-MITZ-vah) Ceremony when a Jewish girl joins the worshiping community (see pp. 36–37).

Batak (BAH-tock) *Church* Christian denomination of the Protestant type (see p. 56).

B.C. Before Christ (see p. 42).

B.C.E. Before the Common Era (see p. 42).

Benares (buh-NAH-ris) Same as **Banaras** (see p. 138).

Bhagavad-Gita (bah-gah-vahd-GEE-tah) Song of the Lord, one of the most famous of the many Hindu holy books (see p. 94).

Bible (BUY-b'l) *1)* Collection of 66 holy books (see pp. 43, 74), honored in whole or part by Jews (see pp. 23, 26, 28–31, 35–36, 193–194), Christians (see pp. 6, 43–51, 60, 62, 64), Muslims (see pp. 73–75), and followers of certain other religions (see pp. 208, 210, 215). *2)* Name used by several Christian denominations of the Protestant type (see p. 56).

birth Different ways of worshiping follow different customs related to birth and childhood (see pp. 37, 65, 88, 107, 121, 133, 157, 171).

bishop Manager or administrator in the organization of many Christian denominations such as the Roman Catholic Church (see pp. 52–53, 63).

bodhisattva (bo-dee-SOT-vah) Person who has reached **enlightenment** but who chooses to stay and help other people instead of passing on into **nirvana** (see pp. 150–151); important in **Mahayana** Buddhism.

born again *1)* Term used by many evangelical Christians to describe what happens to them when they turn the control of their lives over to Jesus Christ (see p. 59). *2)* See **reincarnation** (pp. 99–100, 106, 144, 180).

Boys' Festival Shinto celebration held every May 5 (see p. 131).

Brahma (BRAH-mah) One of the main gods of Hinduism (see p. 97).

Branch Davidian (duh-VID-ih-yun) **Destructive cult** in twentieth-century America (see p. 210).

Brethren (BREH-thrin) Name used by several Christian denominations of the Protestant type (see p. 56).

brother-sister ceremony Joyful ceremony held each August in Sikh households (see p. 183).

Buddha (BOO-dah) "The **Enlightened** One" or "the **Awakened** One", a title given to Prince Siddhartha Gautama, founder of Buddhism (see pp. 134–146, 148–151, 155, 194, 208).

Buddhism (BOO-diz'm) Several related ways of worshiping, all of which look back to the life and teachings of the **Buddha** (see pp. 7, 9, 12, 110, 120, 128–129, 133, 136, 140–157, 167–169).

Bulgarian Orthodox (bull-GAIR-ih-yan OR-tho-docks) Christian denomination of the Orthodox type (see p. 54).

bushido (boo-SHE-doe) List (unwritten at first) of noble attitudes a Japanese warrior was expected to have (see pp. 127–128).

Calvin, John Outstanding Christian leader at the time of the Protestant Reformation (see pp. 55–56).

cantor (KAN-ter) Music leader of a local group of Jewish worshipers (see p. 24).

Cao Dai (chow DIE) **Syncretistic religion** that started in Vietnam during the 1900s (see p. 208).

cargo cults Name given to several new religions that started on islands of the South Pacific during and after World War II (see p. 197).

caste (CAST), ***caste system*** Hindu system of higher and lower classes in human society (see pp. 101–102, 145, 175, 180).

Catholic (KATH-uh-lick) Universal or general; name given to one of the three main types of Christians (see pp. 7, 9, 12–13, 39–40, 52–54, 55, 63).

challah (HAH-lah) Same as **hallah** (see p. 23).

channels People in the New Age movement who are believed to make contact with the spirit world or with special forms of energy (see p. 195).

Chanukah (HAH-noo-kah) Same as **Hanukkah** (see pp. 20, 31–32).

charismatic (care-is-MAT-ick) Anointed, with the special meaning of being **anointed** by the power of God's **Holy Spirit**; name given to a movement among twentieth-century Christians (see pp. 39–40, 58–59).

Children of God *1)* Name Mahatma Gandhi gave to **outcastes** or **untouchables** in the caste system of India (see p. 102). *2)* Twentieth-century **destructive cult** (see pp. 211–212).

Chinese Catholics (KATH-o-licks) Some Chinese Catholics are Roman Catholics; others are members of a different Christian denomination of the Catholic type (see pp. 53–54).

Chinese religion Daoism is sometimes called the Chinese religion, or Chinese folk religion (see pp. 9, 12, 110–112, 118, 120, 207); however, Confucianism is equally a Chinese religion (see pp. 110, 160–170), and Buddhism also became deeply mixed with both of these Chinese ways of worshiping (see pp. 147–148, 151–152).

Christ "The **Anointed** One," a title given to **Jesus**; same as **Messiah** (see pp. 42–43, 47, 50–51, 58, 61, 73–74, 214).

christening (KRIS-in-ning) Giving a name to a baby at the time he or she experiences **baptism** (see pp. 51, 65).

Christian *1)* Follower of Jesus the Christ, or member of one of the many different types of Christian churches (see pp. 7, 12–14, 21, 38–41, 43, 47–65, 68–69, 71, 74–75, 106, 215, 217). *2)* Name used by several Christian denominations of the Protestant type (see p. 56), and at least one Christian denomination of the Orthodox type (see p. 54).

Christian and Missionary Alliance (MISH-uh-nary uh-LIE-ance) Christian denomination of the Protestant type (see p. 56).

Christianity (kris-ti-ANN-uh-ti) The way of the Christ, or the Christian religion (see pp. 6–9, 12–14, 38–65, 192–197, 208, 214–217).

Christian Science **Syncretistic religion** started in America during the 1800s (see pp. 215, 217).

Christmas December 25, when the birth of Jesus the Christ is celebrated (see pp. 43, 194).

Chun Do Kyo (choon doe KYOE) Syncretistic religion in Korea (see p. 208).

church *1)* Particular **denomination** or group of Christians, such as for instance the Roman Catholic Church (see pp. 52–56). *2)* Congregation, or local group of Christians (see pp. 38–41, 192). *3)* Place of worship for Christians (see pp. 38–40, 214–215).

Church of Christ Name used by several Christian denominations of the Protestant type (see p. 56).

Church of God Name used by several Christian denominations of the Protestant type (see p. 56).

circumcised (SUR-come-sized), ***circumcision*** (SUR-come-sizz-yun) Removal of the foreskin of a boy's penis, a ceremony of worship for Jews (see p. 37) and for Muslims (see p. 88).

Commandments, Ten Important laws given by God to Moses (see pp. 28–29, 210).

Communion (kuh-MEW-nyun) Christian ceremony using bread and wine or grape juice; same as the **Lord's Supper** (see pp. 39, 51–52).

communism (KAH-mew-niz'm) System of government and politics that almost seems like a religion for people who follow it (see pp. 55, 110, 117–118, 168–169, 204–205).

confirmation (con-fur-MAY-shun) Ceremony when boys or girls are made *firm* or strong in the religion into which they were born (see pp. 36, 51, 65, 133).

Confucianism (con-FEW-shun-iz'm) Teachings of Confucius or Kong Fuzi, which later became a way of worshiping (see pp. 9, 12, 110, 120, 128–129, 158–171).

Confucius (con-FEW-shus) Name given by Europeans to **Kong Fuzi**, founder of Confucianism (see pp. 160–165, 167, 169–170).

Congregational (con-gre-GAY-shun-ul) Christian denomination of the Protestant type (see p. 56).

Conservative (con-SUR-vuh-tiv) Name describing certain types of Jews (see p. 35), Christians (see pp. 60–62), Muslims (see pp. 81, 83), and followers of other religions, who try to *conserve* or keep or continue the things they consider most important.

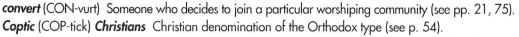

convert (CON-vurt) Someone who decides to join a particular worshiping community (see pp. 21, 75).

Coptic (COP-tick) **Christians** Christian denomination of the Orthodox type (see p. 54).

covenant (KUV-uh-nunt) *1)* Solemn promise; especially, the promise made between God and certain human beings, both in Judaism (see pp. 28–29, 36) and in Christianity (see p. 41). *2)* Name used by some Christian churches and denominations of the Protestant type.

cows, sacred Animals that are especially honored by Hindus in India (see pp. 90, 102).

cross Two crossed pieces of wood, to which a person is nailed to die; the means of execution for common criminals in the time of Jesus (see p. 45). The cross has since become the main symbol of Christianity.

crucifixion (crew-si-FIX-shun) Torture by being nailed to a cross to die (see pp. 45, 47).

Crusades (CREW-sades) Long-ago wars between Christians and Muslims over the ownership of Palestine (see p. 81).

cult *1)* Term sometimes used for almost any way of worshiping that seems new, strange, or different (see pp. 196–197, 211–213). *2)* See **destructive cult** (see pp. 211–213). *3)* See **cargo cults** (see p. 197).

Dao (DOW) Way or path or road or route in Chinese (see pp. 6, 110–111); a basic idea in China and other Asian countries.

Daodejing (dow-day-JING) *The* **Dao** *and Its Power,* an ancient book of poems honored by Daoists (see pp. 113–120).

Daoism (DOW-iz'm) Ancient way of worshiping that started in China (see pp. 6, 9, 12, 108–121, 163–164).

David Great king and hero of ancient times (see pp. 30–31), honored by Jews, Christians, and Muslims.

Dedication (ded-uh-KAY-shun) *1)* Important Jewish festival; same as **Hanukkah** (see pp. 30–31). *2)* Ceremony for babies of Christians who do not baptize babies (see p. 65).

Deepavali (dee-puh-VAH-lee) Festival of Lights, celebrated in the fall each year by Hindus (see p. 96) and by Sikhs (see p. 183).

denominations (dee-nah-muh-NAY-shuns) Different types or groups of Christian churches (see pp. 50, 52–56, 58, 62).

destructive cult Name given to certain newer religions that sometimes become dangerous, or even deadly, for those who follow them and for others as well (see pp. 211–213).

Devi (DAY-vee) General name for several different Hindu goddesses (see p. 99).

devil Leader of the powers of darkness and evil, worshiped by certain people (see pp. 196–197); same as **Satan**.

disciple (dis-SIGH-p'l) *1)* Learner, or one who follows a teacher (see pp. 44, 48, 81, 139–140, 146, 164). *2)* Same as **apostle** (see p. 48). *3)* Same as **Sikh** (see pp. 174, 176). *4)* Name used by a Christian denomination of the Protestant type (see p. 56).

Disciples (dis-SIGH-p'lz) **of Christ** Christian denomination of the Protestant type (see p. 56).

Divine Light Mission Syncretistic religion in twentieth-century America (see pp. 208–209).

Diwali (dee-WAH-lee) Festival of Lights, celebrated each year in the fall by Hindus (see p. 96) and by Sikhs (see p. 183).

Druze (DROOZ) **Syncretistic religion** similar to Islam (see p. 83).

Easter Sunday in springtime celebrating the day when Jesus arose from death (see pp. 43, 45–46).

Eastern Orthodox (OR-tho-docks) Sometimes used as a general name for all Orthodox Christians (see p. 54).

ecumenical (eck-you-MEN-i-k'l) Twentieth-century movement trying to bring different types of Christians closer together (see p. 57).

Eight Steps up the Mountain Basic teachings of Buddhism (see pp. 142–143, 148).

enlightenment (en-LITE-en-ment) Religious experience of **awakening** or inner awareness; a goal to be reached by Hindus (see p. 92), Buddhists (see pp. 138, 146, 149, 150), and Sikhs (p. 180).

Episcopal (ep-ISS-ko-p'l) Christian denomination of the Protestant type (see p. 56).

Ethiopian Orthodox (ee-thee-O-pee-yun OR-tho-docks) Christian denomination of the Orthodox type (see p. 54).

Eucharist (YOU-kuh-rist) Christian ceremony using bread and wine or grape juice; same as the **Lord's Supper** (see pp. 39, 51–52).

evangelical (ee-van-JELL-i-k'l) *1)* Having to do with the good news about Jesus the Christ; used to describe many different kinds of Protestants and other Christians (see pp. 59–60). *2)* Name used by several Christian denominations of the Protestant type (see p. 56).

Five Pillars Five basic things you must believe and do in order to be a Muslim (see pp. 77–79, 82).

Four Noble Truths Basic teachings of Buddhism (see pp. 141–143, 148).

Foursquare Gospel (FOUR-square GAH-sp'l) Christian denomination of the Protestant type (see p. 56).

Friends Christian denomination of the Protestant type; same as **Quakers** (see pp. 52, 56).

Fuji, Mount Snow-capped mountain in Japan, especially important to Shintoists (see p. 132).

fundamentalists (fun-dah-MEN-t'l-ists) Believers who hold strongly to the foundations or *fundamentals* of their faith; used to describe certain Christians (see pp. 60, 62), also certain Muslims (see pp. 81, 83).

Ganesh (gah-NESH), ***Ganesha*** (gah-NESH-ah) One of the main gods of Hinduism (see p. 97).

Ganges (GAN-jeez) Great river in India, believed by Hindus to be sacred (see pp. 92, 107).

Gautama (gah-oo-TAH-mah) Family name of Prince Siddhartha, who later became the Buddha (see pp. 136, 155).

ghetto (GET-toe) Section of a city set aside for Jews (see p. 33).

Girls' Festival Shinto celebration held every March 3 (see pp. 131–132).

Glorious Qur'an (KOO-rahn), ***the*** The Muslims' holy book (see pp. 71–77, 79, 87, 194).

Good Friday Friday in springtime remembering the Friday when Jesus died on the cross (see pp. 43, 45).

Good News Especially, the good news about Jesus Christ; same as **gospel** (see pp. 44–49).

Gospel (GAH-sp'l) *1)* **Good News**, especially the good news about Jesus the Christ (see pp. 44–49). *2)* One of four books in the New Testament telling the good news about Jesus the Christ (see pp. 48–49). *3)* Name used by some Christian churches and denominations of the Protestant type (see p. 56).

Granth (GRAHNT) Holy book of Sikhism (see pp. 175–176, 179–182, 184).

Greek Orthodox (GREEK OR-tho-docks) Christian denomination of the Orthodox type; sometimes used as a general name for all Orthodox Christians (see p. 54).

guru (GOO-roo) *1)* One who gives **enlightenment**, or a religious teacher, especially in the tradition of Hinduism (see pp. 92, 138, 144), Buddhism (see pp. 145–146), and other religions (see pp. 208–209). *2)* Special title for the first ten founding fathers of Sikhism (see pp. 174–177, 181–183).

gurudwara (goo-roo-DWAH-rah) Door of the guru; a Sikh place of worship (see pp. 182, 184).

Guru Granth Sahib (GOO-roo grahnt SAH-eeb) Holy book of Sikhism (see pp. 175–177, 179–182, 184).

Guru Nanak (goo-roo NAH-nock) Founder of Sikhism in the fifteenth century (see pp. 174–176, 181).

hallah (HAH-lah) Braided loaves of bread eaten by Jewish worshipers on the Sabbath Day (see p. 23); same as **challah**.

Hanukkah (HAH-noo-kah) Important Jewish festival in late November or December (see pp. 20, 31–32); same as **Chanukah**.

Hare Krishna (HAH-ray KRISH-nah) Nickname for a twentieth-century movement based on Hinduism (see p. 92).

heaven Term used (especially by Christians) for a higher place, a place of happiness after this life is over (see pp. 47, 71, 78–79, 83, 125, 146).

Hebrew (HE-broo) The Jewish people of ancient times; also, the language they spoke, which has developed into the modern Hebrew language (see p. 22).

hegira (huh-JI-rah) Arabic word meaning flight or escape, referring to the time when Muhammad escaped from Makkah to Medina (see p. 72).

hell Place of punishment after this life is over, believed in by some Jews, many Christians, and all Muslims (see pp. 75, 79).

hijra (HEEJ-rah) Arabic word meaning flight or escape, referring to the time when Muhammad escaped from Makkah to Medina (see p. 72).

Hinayana (hee-nah-YAH-nah) "The Little Ferryboat"; a nickname sometimes used for the **Theravada** type of Buddhism (see pp. 148–151).

Hindu (HINN-doo), **Hinduism** (HINN-doo-iz'm) Ancient way of worshiping that started in India many thousands of years ago (see pp. 7, 9, 90–107, 136, 138, 144–147, 174–177, 180, 183, 207–209).

Hoa Hao (ho-ah HAH-ow) **Syncretistic religion** started in Vietnam during the 1900s (see p. 208).

Holi (HAW-lee) Springtime festival for Hindus (see p. 96) and Sikhs (see p. 183).

Holiness (HOE-li-niss) Name used by several Christian denominations of the Protestant type (see p. 56).

Holocaust (HAH-luh-cost) Complete destruction; a word used for the killing of six million Jews by Hitler and his followers in Europe between 1933 and 1945 (see pp. 33–34).

Holy Bible (BUY-b'l), *the* Collection of 66 holy books (see pp. 43, 74), honored in whole or part by Jews (see pp. 23, 26, 28–31, 35–36, 193–194), Christians (see pp. 6, 43–51, 60, 62, 64), Muslims (see pp. 73–75), and followers of certain other religions (see pp. 208, 210, 215).

Holy Communion (kuh-MEW-nyun), **Holy Eucharist** (YOU-kah-rist) Same as the **Lord's Supper** (see pp. 39, 51–52).

ibadis (ee-BAH-deez) Type of Muslims (see p. 83).

idols (EYE-d'ls)**, idol-gods** Statues or pictures of living beings or other things, used in worship (see pp. 25, 31, 70–71, 73, 96–97).

Idul Fitri (EE-dool FEE-tree) Biggest festival of the year for Muslims (see p. 78).

Iglesia ni Cristo (ee-GLAY-see-ah nee KREES-toe) Twentieth-century religion in the Philippines, similar to Christianity (see p. 214).

images (IM-ij-iz) Statues or pictures of living beings or other things, used in worship (see pp. 96–98, 104, 116, 175, 180).

imam (EE-mom) Leader of Islamic worship (see p. 77); Muslims of the **Shi'ite** type also use this word for some of the founding fathers of their faith, such as **Ali**.

Independent Catholics (KATH-uh-licks) Christian denomination of the Catholic type (see p. 54).

International Society for Krishna (KRISH-nah) **Consciousness** Twentieth-century movement based on Hinduism (see p. 92); same as **Hare Krishna**.

Isaac (EYE-sik) Son of Abraham and Sarah; one of the founding fathers of Judaism (see pp. 25–26, 73).

Ishmael (ISH-may-el) Son of Abraham and Hagar, especially honored by Muslims (see pp. 73, 75).

Islam (ISS-lahm) Arabic word meaning both peace and submission (to the will of God); the Muslim religion (see pp. 7–9, 13–15, 41, 66–88, 105, 174, 177, 194–195, 206–207).

ismailis (ees-mah-EE-leez) Type of Muslims (see p. 83).

Israel (IS-ray-el) **1)** Another name for **Jacob** (see pp. 22, 26). **2)** The Jewish or Hebrew people of ancient times (see pp. 22, 26, 28). **3)** Present-day country in the Middle East (see pp. 21, 22, 34).

Israeli (is-RAY-lee) Citizen of the country of **Israel** (see pp. 22, 34).

Israelite (IS-ray-uh-lite) One of the Jewish people of ancient times (see pp. 22, 26, 28).

Jacob One of the founding fathers of Judaism; also called **Israel** (see pp. 22, 26).

Jain (JINE), **Jainism** (JINE-iz'm) Religion of India, started by **Mahavira** about 500 B.C. (see pp. 202–203).

Japanese religions 1) Shintoism (see pp. 9, 122–133, 207–208). **2)** Many other ways of worshiping, other than Shintoism, have also started in Japan or are followed there today (see pp. 11, 208, 214).

Javanese mysticism (JAH-vah-nees MISS-tuh-siz'm) Several forms of **mysticism** on the Indonesian island of Java (see pp. 203–204).

Jehovah's Witnesses (ji-HOE-vahz WIT-ness-is) Religion similar to Judaism and Christianity, started in America during the 1800s (see pp. 12, 215).

Jerusalem (juh-ROO-suh-lem) City in the Middle East that has special meaning for Jews, Christians, and Muslims; claimed today both by Israelis and by their non-Jewish neighbors (see pp. 25, 31–32, 37, 69, 73).

Jesus Jewish founder of the Christian religion (see pp. 21, 42–50, 61, 201); also honored by Muslims (see pp. 73–74).

Jew, Jewish Words describing people who follow the way of Judaism (see pp. 8–9, 18–37).

Jewish Scriptures (SKRIP-cherz) Holy books of Judaism that are the same in content as the Old Testament in **the Holy Bible** (see pp. 23–31, 35–36, 41–43, 73, 193).

Jimmu Tenno (JIM-moo TEN-noe) First human emperor of Japan in 660 B.C.; Shintoists believe he was a direct descendant of the sun goddess (see pp. 125–126).

John 1) One of Jesus' first followers (see p. 44). 2) The gospel of John, or the good news about Jesus the Christ as written by John—one of the books of the New Testament (see pp. 47–48).

Judah (JOO-dah) One of the founding fathers of Judaism (see pp. 22, 26).

Judaism (JOO-day-izm) The religion of the Jewish people (see pp. 9, 18–37, 42–43, 73–74).

judgment (JUJ-ment) Belief held by some Jews, many Christians (see pp. 46, 213), and all Muslims (see pp. 75, 79), that everyone will be judged at the end of time.

Kaaba (KAH-ah-bah) Cube; an ancient temple in Makkah shaped like a big black block (see pp. 70, 73, 78, 88); Muslims all over the world face toward it when they pray (see pp. 68, 77).

Kali (KAL-lee) One of the main goddesses of Hinduism (see p. 98).

Kami (KAH-mee) Japanese word for "spirits," which also has wider meaning in Shintoism (see pp. 124, 130–133); **Shinto** means the way of the Kami.

Kami-shelf Center of worship in a Shintoist home (see p. 130).

Kardecism (CAR-duh-siz'm) Type of **spiritism** in Brazil (see p. 196).

karma (CAR-mah) The teaching that everything you do—good or bad—will be paid back to you, in this life or the next; believed by Hindus (see p. 99–100), Buddhists (see pp. 144, 157), and Sikhs (see pp. 180–181).

Kimbanguist (kim-BAHNG-oo-ist) **Church** A Christian denomination of the Protestant type (see p. 56).

kitchen god Small image of a god often kept on a special shelf in the kitchen of a Daoist home (see p. 116).

Kong Fu, Kong Fuzi (kong foo ZHUH) Chinese teacher (called **Confucius** by Europeans) who founded Confucianism in about 500 B.C. (see pp. 160–165, 167, 169–170).

Koran (KOO-ran) The Muslims' holy book (see p. 71); a better spelling is **Qur'an**.

Krishna (KRISH-nah) One of the forms in which the Hindu god **Vishnu** is believed to have come to earth (see pp. 92, 102, 208–209).

Lalleswari (lah-less-WAH-ree) Kashmiri woman of the fourteenth century who became a famous Hindu poet (see p. 98).

lama (LAH-mah) Buddhist priest of the Lamaistic type; especially a priest who is believed to be the **reincarnation** of an earlier lama (see pp. 152–154).

Lamaism (LAH-mah-iz'm), **Lamaistic Buddhism** (lah-mah-IS-tick BOO-diz'm) One of the three main types of Buddhism (see pp. 151–154).

Laozi (LAH-oo-tsuh) The Old Master Teacher, who is believed to have written the **Daodejing**; the old form of this name is Lao Tzu (see pp. 113, 160).

Latter-Day Saints Religion similar to Judaism and Christianity, started in America during the 1800s (see pp. 12, 215–217); same as **Mormons**.

Law of Moses Rules and regulations given by God to Moses (including the Ten Commandments); also called **Torah** (see pp. 28–29, 35–37, 41, 210).

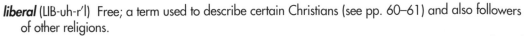

liberal (LIB-uh-r'l) Free; a term used to describe certain Christians (see pp. 60–61) and also followers of other religions.

Lights **1)** Important Jewish festival; same as **Hanukkah** (see pp. 20, 31–32). **2)** Important Hindu and Sikh festival; same as **Diwali** or **Deepavali** (see pp. 96, 183).

Lord's Day Some Christians call Sunday the Lord's Day because they remember that Jesus arose from death on that day (see p. 43).

Lord's Prayer Famous prayer taught by Jesus (see p. 46).

Lord's Resistance Army **Destructive cult** in twentieth-century Uganda (see p. 210).

Lord's Supper Christian ceremony using bread and wine or grape juice (see pp. 39, 51–52); also called Holy **Communion** and Holy **Eucharist**.

Luke **1)** Greek doctor and early follower of Jesus (see pp. 48–49); writer of **Acts**. **2)** The gospel of Luke, or the good news about Jesus the Christ as written by Luke—one of the books of the New Testament (see pp. 48–49).

lunar calendar (LOO-ner KAL-en-dur) Calendar based on when the new moon appears in the sky; used in Judaism (see pp. 18–24), Islam (see pp. 72, 78), and other religions (see pp. 70, 155, 201–202).

Luther, Martin Outstanding Christian leader at the time of the Protestant Reformation (see pp. 55–56).

Lutheran (LOO-thur-un) Name used by several Christian denominations of the Protestant type (see p. 56).

Macumba (mah-KOOM-bah) Type of **spiritism** in Brazil (see p. 196).

Mahavira (mah-hah-VEE-rah) Founder of **Jainism** in about 500 B.C. (see p. 202–203).

Mahayana (mah-hah-YAH-nah) "The Big Ferryboat"; a name used for one of the three main types of Buddhism (see pp. 148, 150–152, 155, 157).

Makkah (muh-KAH) Muslim holy city in Saudi Arabia (see pp. 68–73, 77–78, 87–88, 175); same as **Mecca**.

Mark **1)** Early follower of Jesus (see pp. 48–49). **2)** The gospel of Mark, or the good news about Jesus the Christ as written by Mark—one of the books of the New Testament (see p. 48–49).

marriage Different ways of worshiping have different customs relating to marriage (see pp. 37, 64, 88, 107, 121, 133, 157, 171, 186–187).

Mary of Nazareth Mother of Jesus; same as the **Virgin Mary** (see p. 43).

masjid (MAHS-jeed) Muslim house of worship (see pp. 13–14, 66, 68, 77, 81, 87); same as **mosque**.

mass The main worship service in the Roman Catholic Church that always includes the **Lord's Supper** or **Holy Eucharist** (see pp. 13, 51–52).

Matthew **1)** One of Jesus' first followers (see pp. 44, 49). **2)** The gospel of Matthew, or the good news about Jesus the Christ as written by Matthew—one of the books of the New Testament (see pp. 45–46, 48–49).

Mecca (MECK-uh) **Muslim** holy city in Saudi Arabia (see p. 70); a better spelling and pronunciation is **Makkah**.

medicine man Type of shaman (see pp. 188–190).

Medina (muh-DEE-nuh) Muslim holy city in Saudi Arabia (see pp. 69, 72–73).

meditation (med-uh-TAY-shun) Time of silence and peaceful reflection that is important in many ways of worshiping (see p. 98), especially Buddhism (see pp. 143, 152, 155).

medium In **spiritism**, a person who becomes the means or channel through which other people can get in contact with spirits of the dead (see pp. 188–190, 195–196).

Meng, Mengzi (MUNG, mung-ZUH) Famous Confucian teacher (see p. 165).

Mennonite (MEN-uh-nite) Name used by several Christian denominations of the Protestant type (see p. 56).

menorah (muh-NO-rah) Many-branched candlestick; one of the symbols of modern Judaism (see pp. 18, 31–32).

messenger Term **Muslims** use for the prophet Muhammad because they believe he received a special message from God (see pp. 71, 77, 86).

Messiah (muh-SIGH-yuh) "The Anointed One"; same as **Christ** (see pp. 42–43, 47, 50 51, 214).

Methodist (METH-uh-dist) Name used by several Christian denominations of the Protestant type (see p. 56).

Middle Way Buddhism is sometimes called "the Middle Way" because it doesn't go to extremes in any direction (see pp. 140–141).

minaret (MIN-uh-ret) Steeple or tower of a **masjid**, from which the Muslim call to prayer is sounded five times a day (see pp. 77, 88).

miracle (MEAR-uh-kul) Something that cannot be explained by natural processes (see p. 43).

missionaries (MISH-uh-nair-iz) *1)* Evangelical Christians whose special job is spreading the good news about Jesus the Christ (see pp. 51, 57, 59–60). *2)* Followers of any religion who go out to spread their way of worshiping (see pp. 147–148, 165, 183, 216).

moderate (MAH-dur-it) Word used to describe certain twentieth-century Christians of different denominations (see pp. 60, 62).

Mogen David (MO-gen DAY-vid) Shield of David; a six-pointed star that has become one of the symbols of modern Judaism (see pp. 30, 34). Same as **Star of David**.

Mohammed (moe-HAM-med) Arab religious leader of the sixth century who brought Islam to the world (see pp. 66, 68); a better spelling and pronunciation is **Muhammad**.

monk Unmarried man who separates himself from ordinary life in order to give his whole life to his way of worshiping; there are monks among Roman Catholics, Orthodox Christians, Buddhists, and followers of other religions.

monotheistic religion (MAH-nuh-the-is-tik ree-LIJ-un) Religion that believes in only one God (see pp. 8–9); Judaism (see pp. 25, 37, 193–194), Christianity (see p. 47), and Islam (see pp. 71–72) are monotheistic religions, and some people would include Sikhism as well (see pp. 179–180).

Moonies Nickname for members of the **Unification Church** (see p. 214).

Moravian (moe-RAY-vi-yun) Christian denomination of the Protestant type (see p. 56).

Mormons (MAWR-muns) Same as **Latter-Day Saints** (see pp. 12, 215–217).

Moses Great leader and law-giver of the Jewish people in ancient times (see pp. 26–29, 35–37).

Moslem (MAHS-lum) One who submits; a person who worships in the way of Islam (see pp. 13–14, 66, 68, 75); a better spelling and pronunciation is **Muslim**.

mosque (MAHSK) Muslim house of worship (see pp. 13–14, 66, 68, 77, 81, 87); same as **masjid**.

Mount Fuji Snow-capped mountain in Japan, especially important to Shintoists (see p. 132).

Muhammad (moo-HAHM-mahd) "One who is highly praised"; Arab religious leader of the sixth century who brought Islam to the world (see pp. 15, 66, 68, 70–74); same as **Mohammed**.

Muslim (MOOS-lim) One who submits; a person who worships in the way of Islam (see pp. 7–9, 13–15, 34, 66–88, 105, 174–177, 194–195, 206–207); same as **Moslem**.

mysticism (MISS-tuh-siz'm) Spiritual experiences going beyond the mind or the five senses, an important part of religion for followers of many different ways of worshiping (see pp. 203–204).

myth **1)** Ancient story explaining how things got started or why things are as they are today (see p. 190). **2)** Something that doesn't really exist (p. 190).

Nanak, Guru (GOO-roo NAH-nock) Founder of Sikhism in the fifteenth century (see pp. 174–176, 181).

Nation of Islam, The American Islamic group in the twentieth century, not considered truly Muslim by certain Muslims in other countries (see pp. 14, 86, 217).

Native American religions The **primal religions** of Native American tribes. Some of the tribes still practice these religions (see p. 192).

Nativity (nuh-TIV-uh-ti) Birth, especially the birth of Jesus in Bethlehem (see pp. 43, 201).

Nazarenes (NAZ-uh-reenz) Christian denomination of the Protestant type (see p. 56).

New Age movement Name given to several different twentieth-century religions that seem similar in some ways to **animism** and **spiritism** (see pp. 195–196).

new religions General term used for many of the newer ways of worshiping (see pp. 214–217).

New Testament (TES-tuh-ment) The last 27 books of **the Holy Bible,** telling about Jesus and his first followers (see pp. 41, 43, 45–49); Christians and Muslims honor the New Testament as holy books, but Jewish worshipers do not (see p. 74).

new year Time for important festivals in many religions, including Judaism (see pp. 20, 24–25), Islam (see pp. 72, 78), Daoism (see p. 118), and Shintoism (see p. 131).

nirvana (near-VAH-nah) Final goal of the Buddhist way of worshiping (see pp. 146–147, 150).

Noble Truths, Four Basic teachings of Buddhism (see pp. 141–143, 148).

nun Unmarried woman who separates herself from ordinary life in order to give her whole life to her way of worshiping; there are nuns among Roman Catholics, Buddhists, and followers of other religions.

Obeah (o-BAY-uh) Type of **spiritism** in Jamaica (see p. 196).

occult (ock-KULT) General term for **spiritism** and for religions that have to do with witches, Satan, the devil, or the powers of darkness and evil (see p. 197).

Old Testament (TES-tuh-ment) The first 39 books of **the Holy Bible,** telling about Abraham, Moses, King David, and other people honored by Jews, Christians, and Muslims (see pp. 23–31, 35–36, 41–43, 73, 193); the same in content as the **Jewish Scriptures**.

Orthodox (OR-tho-docks) Right worship; a word used to describe one type of Judaism (see p. 35) and one type of Christianity (see pp. 54–55); also used to describe certain Muslims and other worshipers who want to follow strictly the "right" ways.

outcastes (OUT-casts) People of India who are considered to be of such a low level in society that they fall below the lowest **caste** (see pp. 101–102).

pagan (PAY-g'n) **paganism** (PAY-gun-iz'm) Worship of ancient gods and goddesses in ancient ways (see p. 193).

parables (PAIR-uh-bulz) Stories with hidden or symbolic meanings, especially the stories told by Jesus (see p. 44).

paradise (PAIR-uh-dice) Term used (especially by Muslims) for a place of happiness after this life is over (see pp. 79, 83).

Parsi (PAR-see) Persian; a name given to **Zoroastrianism** (see p. 202).

partisans (PAR-tuh-sunz) Root meaning in Arabic of the word **Shi'ites**, because Shi'ite Muslims take the *part* of **Ali** and his descendants (see pp. 82–83, 85).

Passover (PASS-o-vur) Important Jewish festival in the spring of every year (see pp. 20, 22, 26–28).

pastor (PASS-tur) Shepherd; a name used for the leader of a local group of Christians, especially among Protestants (see pp. 56, 65).

patriarchs (PAY-tri-arks) *1)* Founding fathers of Judaism, including Abraham, Isaac, and Jacob or Israel (see pp. 25–26). *2)* Several top-level church leaders among Orthodox Christians (p. 54).

Paul Follower and **apostle** of Jesus Christ who became the outstanding Christian leader of ancient times; writer of many important letters that are now books in the New Testament (see pp. 48–49, 65).

Pentecostal (PEN-ti-cost-t'l) Name used by several Christian denominations of the Protestant type (see p. 56).

People of the Book Term used by the Prophet Muhammad for Jews and Christian because both of these ways of worshiping had holy books (see p. 74).

Peoples Temple **Destructive cult** of the twentieth century (see p. 180).

philosophy (fuh-LAH-suh-fih) A particular way of thinking or of looking at life; some people say Daoism is not really a religion but a philosophy (see p. 116).

pilgrims People who travel to a particular place because of their religion (see pp. 70, 78, 92, 107, 132).

Pillars, Five Five basic things you must believe and do in order to be a Muslim (see pp. 77–79, 82).

pogrom (PO-grum) Campaign to wipe out all Jewish people in a certain place (see pp. 33–34).

Pope Papa or father; the bishop of Rome, who is the supreme leader of the Roman Catholic Church (see pp. 53, 63).

Presbyterian (prez-bih-TIER-i-yun) Name used by several Christian denominations of the Protestant type (see p. 56).

priest (PREEST) Religious leader, especially one who offers **sacrifices**; there are priests among Roman Catholics (see pp. 56, 65), Orthodox Christians, Hindus (see pp. 95, 104), Daoists (see pp. 112, 116, 118), Shintoists (see pp. 130, 133), Buddhists (see p. 133), Confucianists (see p. 168), and followers of other ways of worshiping.

primal (PRY-mul) **religions** First religions; the oldest ways of worshiping (see pp. 186–197, 208).

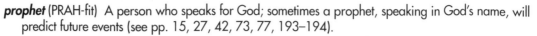

prophet (PRAH-fit) A person who speaks for God; sometimes a prophet, speaking in God's name, will predict future events (see pp. 15, 27, 42, 73, 77, 193–194).

Protestant (PRAH-tes-tunt) One who *protests*; name given to one of the three main types of Christians (see pp. 55–56, 58–60, 62).

Protestant Reformation (PRAH-tes-tunt ref-or-MAY-shun) Movement that began in the sixteenth century as a *protest* against the Roman Catholic Church; nearly all Protestant denominations grew out of this movement (see pp. 55–56).

Psalms (SAHMZ) Ancient Jewish hymns of praise (see p. 30); also used and honored by Christians and Muslims.

puja (POO-jah) Daily worship services, performed either at home or at a temple, by Hindus (see pp. 96, 104) or by Buddhists (pp. 154–155).

Purim (POO-reem) Important Jewish festival (see pp. 20, 31).

Quakers (KWAY-kerz) Christian denomination of the Protestant type; same as **Friends** (see pp. 52, 56).

Qur'an (KOO-ran) The Muslims' holy book (see pp. 71–77, 79, 87, 194); same as **Koran**.

rabbi (RAB-bye) Spiritual leader, teacher, and counselor of a local group of Jewish worshipers (see p. 24).

Rabi'a (rah-BEE-uh) Muslim woman of the eighth century who became a famous Sufi poet (see pp. 83–84).

Rama (RAH-mah) One of the forms in which the Hindu god Vishnu is believed to have come to earth (see p. 94).

Ramayana (rah-mah-YAH-nah) One of the most famous of the many Hindu holy books (see p. 94).

Rastafarian, (ras-tuh-FAIR-i-yun), **Rastafarianism** (ras-tuh-FAIR-i-yun-iz'm) **Syncretistic religion** for people of African descent (see p. 208).

Reform (rih-FORM) Word used to describe one type of Judaism (see p. 35).

Reformation (ref-or-MAY-shun) Protestant movement that began in the sixteenth century as a protest against the Roman Catholic Church; nearly all present-day Protestant denominations grew out of this movement (see pp. 55–56).

Reformed (rih-FORMD) Name used by several Christian denominations of the Protestant type (see p. 56).

reincarnation (ree-in-car-NAY-shun) Belief of Hindus, Buddhists, Sikhs, and others, that a person who dies is then reborn into another body (see pp. 99–100, 102, 106, 144, 153, 180).

Religion of Three's **Syncretistic religion** on the Indonesian island of Lombok (see p. 208).

resurrection (reh-sur-RECK-shun) Rising from death; especially the rising of Jesus from death (see pp. 43, 45–46, 54, 64).

Roman Catholic (roe-mun KATH-uh-lick) Largest Christian denomination, recognizing the Pope, the bishop of Rome, as its spiritual leader (see pp. 7, 13, 39–40, 52–53).

Rosh Hashanah (ROASH hah-sha-NAH) Head of the year; an important Jewish new year's festival (see pp. 20, 24).

Russian Orthodox (RUSH-yun OR-tho-docks) Christian denomination of the Orthodox type; sometimes used as a general name for all **Orthodox** Christians (see pp. 54–55).

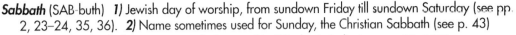

Sabbath (SAB-buth) *1)* Jewish day of worship, from sundown Friday till sundown Saturday (see pp. 2, 23–24, 35, 36). *2)* Name sometimes used for Sunday, the Christian Sabbath (see p. 43)

sacred cows Animals that are especially honored by Hindus in India (see pp. 90, 102).

sacred string Initiation ceremony into the worshiping community for a Hindu boy (see pp. 103, 174–175).

sacrifice (SACK-ri-fice) Act of worship in several different religions that involves offering something or giving something up to be killed or destroyed (see pp. 24–25, 47, 73, 75, 78, 95–96, 112, 118, 189, 196).

Salvation (sal-VAY-shun) **Army** Christian denomination of the Protestant type (see p. 56).

Santeria (sahn-tuh-REE-ah) Type of **spiritism** in Cuba (see p. 196).

Satan (SAY-t'n) Leader of the powers of darkness and evil, worshiped by certain people (see p. 196); same as the **devil**.

Savior, Saviour (SAVE-yer) One who saves; especially refers to Jesus the Christ (see pp. 42, 50, 56, 61, 74).

Scriptures (SKRIP-cherz) Holy writings, such as the **Jewish Scriptures** (see pp. 23–31, 35–36, 41–43, 73, 193), **the Holy Bible** (see pp. 6, 43–51, 60, 62, 64), **the Glorious Qur'an** (see pp. 71–77, 79, 87, 194), and holy books of other religions (see pp. 94, 100, 141, 145, 149, 153–154, 175–177, 179–182, 184, 190).

Serbian Orthodox (SUR-bi-yun OR-tho-docks) Christian denomination of the Orthodox type (see p. 54).

Shakti (SHOCK-tee) General name for several different Hindu goddesses (see p. 99).

shalom (shah-LOAM) Peace; a Hebrew word that is also the root word for **Islam** in Arabic (see pp. 68–69, 74).

shaman (SHAH-mun) Religious leader believed to have special power or knowledge (see pp. 188–190, 192).

shamanism (SHAH-mun-iz'm) Religion led by a **shaman** (see pp. 188–190, 192).

Shavuot (SHAH-voo-awt) Important Jewish festival (see pp. 20, 29).

Shelters Important Jewish festival; same as **Sukkot** (see pp. 20, 28).

Shi'a, Shi'ah (SHE-ah) Same as **Shi'ites** (see pp. 82–83, 85).

Shield of David Six-pointed star that has become one of the symbols of modern Judaism (see pp. 30–34). Same as **Star of David**.

Shi'ites (SHE-ites) One of the two major types of Muslims (see pp. 82–83, 85); same as **Shi'a** or **Shi'ah**.

Shinto (SHIN-toe), **Shintoism** (SHIN-toe-iz'm) The Way of the **Kami**; an ancient way of worshiping that is still the main religion of Japan (see pp. 9, 122–133, 207–208).

Shiva (SHE-vah) The Hindu god who creates life but also destroys it (see pp. 97, 99).

shofar (SHOW-far) Curved trumpets made of animal horns, blown once a year in the Jewish worship service of **Rosh Hashanah** (see p. 24).

shrine (SHRINE) Place of worship (see pp. 154–155), especially in Shintoism (pp. 128, 130–133).

Siddhartha (see-DAR-thah) Name of the prince who later became the **Buddha** (see pp. 134–138, 155, 161).

Sikh (SEEK), *Sikhism* (SEEK-iz'm) Religion started by **Guru Nanak** in the fifteenth century (see pp. 172–184, 206–207).

Simchat Torah (SIM-cot TOE-rah) Rejoicing over the **Torah**; an important Jewish festival (see pp. 20, 28).

Soka Gakkai (so-kah GOCK-eye) Type of **Mahayana** Buddhism in Japan (see p. 152).

Son of God Title for Jesus the **Christ**—a way of trying to explain who he really is (see pp. 47, 61).

spiritism (SPEAR-it-iz'm) Several different religions that involve contact with spirits of the dead (see pp. 188–189, 195–197).

spirits Many spirits live in this world, according to those who follow the way of the Dao (see pp. 112, 116), the Shinto way (see pp. 124–125, 128–132), and many other religions (see pp. 188–189, 195–197).

spiritualism (SPEAR-it-chool-iz'm) Same as **spiritism** (see pp. 188–189, 195–197).

Star of David Six-pointed star that has become one of the symbols of modern Judaism (see pp. 30, 34).

Steps up the Mountain, Eight Basic teachings of Buddhism (see pp. 142–143, 148).

Subud (SOO-bood) Twentieth-century **syncretistic religion**; one type of Javanese **mysticism** (see pp. 203–204).

Sufi (SOO-fee) Certain Muslims who say that inner feelings or spiritual things are what is most important in religion (see pp. 83–84).

Sukkot (SUH-kawt) **Shelters**; an important Jewish festival (see pp. 20, 28).

sun goddess One of the **Kami**. Shintoists believe that each Japanese emperor is a direct descendant of the sun goddess (see pp. 125–126, 129, 132).

Sunday Day of worship for most Christians, since Jesus arose from death on a Sunday (see p. 43).

Sunni (SOO-nee), *Sunnites* (SOO-nites) One of the two major types of Muslims (see pp. 13–14, 83).

Swiss Order of the Solar Temple **Destructive cult** in twentieth-century Switzerland and Canada (see p. 210).

synagogue (SIN-uh-gog) Ancient name for a Jewish house of worship, still used by Orthodox Jews today (see p. 35).

syncretism (SIN-creh-tiz'm), *syncretistic* (sin-creh-TISS-tick) *religion* Mix-and-match religions, or ways of worshiping that seem to be somewhat like two or more other religions (see pp. 207–209).

Tao (DOW), *Taoism* (DOW-iz'm) Older spellings for **Dao** and **Daoism** (see p. 110).

Tao Te Ching (DOW-deh-jing) Older spelling for **Daodejing** (see p. 113).

Techno-pagans (teck-no-PAY-guns) Pagans who use computers to meet together and worship through the Internet (see p. 193).

Temple **1)** Main Jewish house of worship that used to stand in Jerusalem (see pp. 25, 31–32, 37). **2)** Any Reform Jewish house of worship today (p. 35). **3)** The Sikhs' holiest place, the Golden Temple in Amritsar, India (see pp. 177–178). **4)** Any house of worship, especially of Hinduism (see pp. 95–96, 98, 104), Daoism (see pp. 112, 116, 118–119), Buddhism (see pp. 148, 155–157), or Confucianism (see p. 168), or other religions (see p. 216).

Ten Commandments Important laws given by God to Moses (see pp. 28–29, 143–144, 210).

testament (TES-tuh-ment) *1)* Same as **covenant** (see p. 41). *2)* One of the two parts of **the Holy Bible**: The Old Testament and the New Testament (see p. 41).

theistic (thee-IS-tick) *religion* Way of worshiping whose followers believe in a personal god (see p. 179).

Theosophy (thee-OSS-uh-fih) **Syncretistic religion** in the United States during the nineteenth and twentieth centuries (see pp. 208–209).

Theravada (thear-uh-VAH-dah) The Way of the Elders; the name used by one of the three main types of Buddhism (see pp. 148–151, 157); also called **Hinayana** (see p. 148).

3HO Foundation Healthy, Happy, Holy Organization, which helps spread Sikhism in the United States (see p. 183).

tolerance (TAH-ler-unce) Attitude of "live and let live," or not interfering with those who follow a different way of worshiping (see pp. 105–106).

Torah (TOE-ruh) The first five books of the **Jewish Scriptures** (see pp. 28–29, 36); also the whole way of life of Judaism.

torii (TOE-ree-ee) Gateway to a Japanese shrine; it has become the symbol of Shintoism (see p. 132).

Tripitaka (trih-pih-TAH-kah) Three baskets; the oldest Buddhist Scriptures (see p. 149).

Umbanda (oom-BAHN-dah) Type of **spiritism** in Brazil (see p. 196).

Unification (you-nif-uh-KAY-shun) *Church* Religion similar to Christianity, started in South Korea in the twentieth century; same as **Moonies** (see pp. 12, 214, 216).

Unitarian Universalists (you-nuh-TAIR-ih-yun you-nuh-VUR-sul-ists) Religion (similar to Judaism and Christianity) in the United States during the nineteenth and twentieth centuries (see p. 215).

Unity (YOU-nuh-tih) *School of Christianity* **Syncretistic religion** in twentieth-century America (see p. 215).

untouchables (un-TOUCH-uh-b'lz) People of India who are considered to be of such a low level in society that they fall below the lowest **caste** (see pp. 101–102).

Varanasi (vah-rah-NAH-see) Same as **Banaras** (see p. 138).

Vedanta (veh-DON-tah) *Society* **Syncretistic religion** in the United States during the nineteenth and twentieth centuries (see pp. 208–209).

Vedas (VAY-duz) Hymns to gods and goddesses, the oldest of the many Hindu holy books (see p. 94).

Virgin Mary Mary of Nazareth, mother of Jesus; so called because she was believed to have given birth to Jesus without having had a sexual partner (see p. 43).

Vishnu (VISH-noo) The Hindu god who preserves life (see pp. 94, 99, 102).

Voodoo (VOO-doo) Type of **spiritism** found in Africa, Haiti, and elsewhere (see pp. 196–197).

Wahhabis (wah-HAH-bees) Type of Muslims (see p. 83).

wedding Different ways of worshiping follow different wedding customs (see pp. 37, 64, 88, 107, 121, 133, 157, 171, 186–187).

Weeks Important Jewish festival; same as **Shavuot** (see pp. 20, 29).

Wesleyan (WES-li-yun) Christian denomination of the Protestant type (see p. 56).

witch doctor Nickname for a **shaman** (see pp. 188–190).

Word of Life Church Christian denomination of the Protestant type (see p. 56).

World War II A war that took place from 1939–1945. Shintoism had a strong effect on this war, and this war—especially the way it ended—had a strong effect on Shintoism (see pp. 129–130). Also, World War II caused the starting of several so-called **cargo cults** on several islands in the South Pacific (see p. 197).

worship How we give honor and recognition to that which we consider to be of highest worth or value (see p. 5).

yang (YAHNG), **yin** (YEEN) Two kinds of energy at work in the world, according to Daoism (see pp. 111–112) and Confucianism (see pp. 162–163); a basic idea in China and other Asian countries.

yoga (YO-gah) One form of the Hindu way of worshiping (see p. 95).

Yom Kippur (yawm KEE-pur) Day of Atonement; an important Jewish new year's festival (see pp. 20, 24–25).

Zarathushtra (zah-rah-TOOS-trah) Founder of **Zoroastrianism** (or the **Parsi** religion), who lived perhaps as early as 1400 B.C.; same as **Zoroaster** (see pp. 201, 208).

Zen Form of Mahayana Buddhism popular in Japan and the United States (see pp. 152, 155).

zodiac (ZOE-di-ack) Method of deciding the relative positions of the planets, sun, moon, and stars; important in astrology (see pp. 201–202).

Zoroaster (zoe-roe-AST-ur) Same as **Zarathushtra** (see p. 201).

Zoroastrianism (zoe-roe-AST-ri-yun-iz'm) Ancient way of worshiping started by Zarathushtra perhaps as early as 1400 B.C.; same as the **Parsi** religion (see pp. 201–202).